Canadian Harvest Cookbook

Sayers • Darcy

CANADA COOKS

Canadian Harvest Cookbook

Copyright © Company's Coming Publishing Limited

First Printing September 2014

Library and Archives Canada Cataloguing in Publication

Sayers, 1975-, author

The Canadian harvest cookbook / Jennifer Sayers, James Darcy.

(Canada cooks series)

Includes index.

Originally published: Edmonton : Lone Pine Publishing, 2008.

ISBN 978-1-927126-71-4 (pbk.)

1. Cooking, Canadian. 2. Local foods--Canada. 3. Farm produce--Canada. 4. Cookbooks. I. Darcy, James, author II. Title. III. Series: Canada cooks series

TX715.6.B347 2014	641.5971	C2014-900821-X

Cover photo: Lorthios / Photocuisine

Published by

Company's Coming Publishing Limited

87 Pender Street East

Vancouver, British Columbia, Canada V6A 1S9

www.companyscoming.com

Company's Coming is a registered trademark owned by Company's Coming Publishing Limited

We acknowledge the financial support of the Government of Canada through the Canada Book Fund for our publishing activities.

Printed in China

PC: 25

CONTENTS

The Company's Coming Story

Jean Paré (pronounced "jeen PAIR-ee") grew up understanding that the combination of family, friends and home cooking is the best recipe for a good life. When Jean left home, she took with her a love of cooking, many family recipes and an intriguing desire to read cookbooks as if they were novels!

When her four children had all reached school age, Jean volunteered to cater the 50th anniversary celebration of the Vermilion School of Agriculture, now Lakeland College, in Alberta, Canada. Working out of her home, Jean prepared a dinner for more than 1,000 people, launching a flourishing catering operation that continued for over 18 years.

"Never share a recipe you wouldn't use yourself."

As requests for her recipes increased, Jean was often asked the question, "Why don't you write a cookbook?" The publication of *150 Delicious Squares* on April 14, 1981 marked the debut of what would soon become one of the world's most popular cookbook series.

Company's Coming cookbooks are distributed in Canada, the United States, Australia and other world markets. Bestsellers many times over in English, Company's Coming cookbooks have also been published in French and Spanish.

Familiar and trusted in home kitchens around the world, Company's Coming cookbooks are offered in a variety of formats. Highly regarded as kitchen workbooks, the softcover Original Series, with its lay-flat plastic comb binding, is still a favourite among readers.

Jean Paré's approach to cooking has always called for *quick and easy recipes* using *everyday ingredients.* That view has served her well.

Jean continues to share what she calls The Golden Rule of Cooking: *Never share a recipe you wouldn't use yourself.* It's an approach that has worked—*millions of times over!*

Nutrition Information Guidelines

Each recipe is analyzed using the most current version of the Canadian Nutrient File from Health Canada, which is based on the United States Department of Agriculture (USDA) Nutrient Database.

- If more than one ingredient is listed (such as "butter or hard margarine"), or if a range is given (1 – 2 tsp., 5 – 10 mL), only the first ingredient or first amount is analyzed.

- For meat, poultry and fish, the serving size per person is based on the recommended 4 oz. (113 g) uncooked weight (without bone), which is 2 – 3 oz. (57 – 85 g) cooked weight (without bone)— approximately the size of a deck of playing cards.

- Milk used is 1% M.F. (milk fat), unless otherwise stated.

- Cooking oil used is canola oil, unless otherwise stated.

- Ingredients indicating "sprinkle," "optional," or "for garnish" are not included in the nutrition information.

- The fat in recipes and combination foods can vary greatly depending on the sources and types of fats used in each specific ingredient. For these reasons, the amount of saturated, monounsaturated and polyunsaturated fats may not add up to the total fat content.

INTRODUCTION

Night begins to fall a little earlier, the sky turns a slightly deeper shade of blue than it has been all summer long and the air feels just a little fresher: autumn has arrived. You can smell it in the air. We can't help but mourn, just a little, the passing of another summer, but autumn has its own delights to offer. The crisp air is energizing as we walk among brightly coloured foliage, and we look forward to the first snowfall.

There are corn mazes to run through and hay wagons to ride, apples to pick and pumpkin festivals to attend. Also, Thanksgiving and Hallowe'en are just on the horizon. Country fairs are held across Canada, where those of us with a competitive streak show off the best of our garden's crop along with the fruits of our labours in the kitchen.

Outside, we're busy bringing in the last of the garden's bounty, tidying the yard, and perhaps planting trees and bulbs in anticipation of spring. Inside, we're busy, too, preserving the last of the goodies from the garden so they will last just a little bit longer. As we enjoy the last of the tomatoes, berries, melons and other summer crops, we welcome the appearance of apples, pears, nuts, squash and root vegetables sweetened by frost.

Endive, Pear and Walnut Salad with Rosemary Vinaigrette, p. 40.

Cranberry Tartlets, p. 148.

Along with new ingredients, we embrace the return of cool-weather cooking techniques: delicious aromas drift through the house; the stove stays on longer, slow-cooking soups and stews; and the oven returns to its role as the star of the kitchen, baking, braising and roasting.

Our harvest cookbook is a celebration of autumn in the kitchen. It starts in your garden or at your local farmers' market with fresh ingredients, grown as close to your home as you can get. The diversity of the Canadian landscape translates into variety in our harvest, which continues all the way onto our tables. And if frost comes a little sooner to us than to other parts of the world, it only makes our carrots and our beets that much sweeter.

In Canada, diversity also refers to our cultural heritage. Because of this, Canadian cuisine can be one of the most difficult in the world to define. Our dishes draw on a variety of cultural influences, from First Nations foodways to Scottish, Italian, Asian or classic French cuisine. Cooked in our kitchens with ingredients grown, raised or fished in our country, all of this is Canadian cooking.

You'll find creative ideas for cooking with our country's best seasonal ingredients such as wild mushrooms, cider, game meats, squash and root vegetables, as well as some, such as maple syrup, which may not be harvested at this time of year but taste like autumn anyway. Start with the best raw ingredients and you'll taste the difference in the finished dish.

All of our recipes have been tested in our kitchen, so you can expect delicious results, even if you're cooking something for the first time. For the best results, be sure to read through the other sections of our introduction. "In Our Kitchen" provides details of some of the conventions of our test kitchen that may be assumed in the text of the recipes. "Essential Ingredients" describes the types and uses of many of the basics.

We've included a range of recipes, from familiar comfort foods with a twist and simple, quick dishes for a weeknight or a day you'd rather spend outside, to more elaborate dishes for entertaining or for when the spirit of culinary adventure strikes. Whether you're looking for one new dish to pair with your own favourite recipes or for an entire menu from appetizers through to desserts and midnight snacks, you'll find it in these pages.

Wild and White Rice Pilaf with Dried Cranberries, p. 86.

Pumpkin Mousse, p. 152.

Gingerbread Bread Puddings, p. 144.

In Our Kitchen

We have found the following ingredient choices and cooking procedures to be successful in our kitchen and recommend them highly wherever possible.

Butter is unsalted and is easiest to measure using the convenient markings on the wrapping.

Citrus juices are fresh squeezed.

Eggs are large, free-range eggs. They should be at room temperature for baking.

Flour is unbleached all-purpose.

Herbs are fresh, unless stated otherwise. In a pinch, the best alternative to fresh is frozen. You can freeze herbs yourself in the summer when they are plentiful, and you can even find them in the freezer section of some grocery stores.

Mushrooms, such as morels and chanterelles, can be found in the wild, but we advise that you confirm the identification of mushrooms with an experienced collector before cooking them; some species are acutely toxic and can cause death.

Stocks are homemade. Good quality stocks in cans or asceptic boxes are the best substitute. Avoid using those nasty little cubes and powders. Miso, a fermented soybean paste, is another interesting alternative to stock, and it will keep in the refrigerator for several months. Stir it in, 1 Tbsp (15 mL) at a time, until you have a rich, full flavour.

Sugar is organic and unrefined rather than white and bleached. When looking for a rich brown sugar, use muscovado sugar, available in grocery and health food stores. It retains the minerals and vitamins originally in the sugar cane plant, and it has a full molasses flavour.

Yeast is regular dry yeast; 1/2 oz (15 mL) dry yeast is equal to 1 Tbsp (15 mL) fresh yeast.

Measuring

Dry ingredients should be spooned into the measuring cup and leveled off with a knife or spatula.

Solids, including butter and most cheeses, are measured in dry-measure cups and liquids in liquid-measure cups.

Essential Ingredients

The following ingredients are used in many of the recipes in this book; special ingredients found in just one or two recipes are described where they are used. Some items are widely available, whereas others are best sought in gourmet, specialty food, health food or ethnic stores or obtained by mail order or the Internet.

Bay Leaves— Fresh leaves have such a different flavour that they are worth the effort to find. They are occasionally available at large grocery stores and can be specially ordered. In a well-sealed container in the fridge, they can last three or four months.

Coconut Milk—Use unsweetened coconut milk in cans. Naturally sweet, it is often better than cream in savory dishes.

Garlic—Use fresh garlic! An Italian friend says that if you can't be bothered to peel and chop fresh garlic you shouldn't be allowed to use it!

Lemons and Limes—Use fresh! You can't compare the taste to concentrate.

Mayonnaise—It's always better homemade:

5 egg yolks

1/4 cup (60 mL) good quality vinegar or juice from 1 lemon

pinch of sea salt to taste

2/3 cup (150 mL) extra virgin olive oil

- You need both hands free to make mayonnaise. Spread a damp cloth on your counter, nestle a medium-sized bowl in its centre and wrap it around the base of the bowl to keep it steady while you whisk.

- Whisk yolk, vinegar and salt in bowl until well combined and yolk has lightened in colour.

- Add oil, a drop at a time, whisking continuously until mixture emulsifies and thickens.

- When about half of oil has been added, whisk in remaining oil in a slow, steady stream. Store, covered, in refrigerator for up to five days. You can thin your mayonnaise by lightly whisking in some water.

- Many people like to add mustard or fresh herbs to their mayonnaise. Adding minced garlic turns plain mayonnaise into aioli. Makes just over 1 cup (250 mL).

This page: Brussels Sprout Leaf Salad with Bacon Vinaigrette, p. 44; Opposite page: White Bean Roasted Vegetable Soup, p. 34.

Mustard—Use good quality mustard for everything from sandwiches to dressings to sauces. When you are down to the last few drops clinging to the bottom and sides of your mustard jar, add fresh lemon juice, olive oil, sea salt and fresh pepper for a yummy impromptu salad dressing. Just shake and enjoy.

Oil, Sesame—Use for a nutty flavour addition. Store in the fridge.

Oil, Olive—Extra virgin olive oil is indispensable. Try olive oil from Italy, Spain or Greece.

Oil, Grape Seed—Use for higher heat cooking.

Pepper, Fresh—Freshly ground pepper has a far superior flavour to pre-ground, which loses a lot of its pungency and spice. A variety of peppercorns are available. Black or white pepper can be used interchangeably in any of the recipes, although their flavour is slightly different.

Peppers—When handling hot peppers, wear plastic or rubber gloves to avoid capsaicin burns. Capsaicin is the compound in all varieties of pepper (except bell peppers) that gives them their heat, and it is easily transferred through skin-to-skin contact. If you decide to live dangerously and forego the gloves, make sure you wash your hands thoroughly before touching your face, eyes or loved ones.

Salt—Great salt is the key to great cooking. Salt brings out the flavour in food. There are many amazing salts in the world to reach for—sea salt, kosher salt or flavoured salts—choose a favourite. Better yet, obtain some of each. Regular salt can have a chemical aftertaste, and using a better quality salt also means that you will use less, because the flavour is more intense. If you need to reduce salt even further for health reasons, use fresh herbs, various spices and flavour lifters such as lemon juice to maintain the intensity while reducing the salt content.

Soy Sauce—Both tamari and shoyu are high quality, fermented and chemical-free sauces that are used to enhance flavour and impart a unique saltiness.

Star Anise—This strongly anise-scented Oriental spice is commonly sold dried, as quarter-sized, star-shaped clusters of 5 to 10 pods, each containing a single seed. The seeds can be used on their own, crushed or ground, or the entire stars can be added, then removed.

Vinegar, Apple Cider—Organic, unrefined and unpasteurized apple cider vinegar has the best flavour.

Vinegar, Balsamic—Balsamic vinegar is an aged reduction sauce that originates in the Modena region of Italy. It adds a deep, rich yet piquant, flavour to everything from soups to sweets. White balsamic vinegar is a pale gold variation that is not caramelized during processing and is not aged as long as regular balsamic vinegar. It is used in salads but can also be used in pale sauces served with a variety of meats, poultry and seafood.

Toasted Pumpkin Seeds Two Ways

Serves 10

We use pumpkin seeds in this recipe, but you can toast the seeds of any variety of winter squash with the same delicious results. The seeds are actually one of the most nutritious parts of these Native American fruits, containing high levels of zinc and iron. If you prefer to forego the added crunch of the hulls, you can use hulled pumpkin seeds, known as pepitas, to make this recipe. The egg white in the coating of our recipe binds the spices to the seeds so the flavour doesn't end up left in the bottom of the bowl. You will need parchment paper for this recipe.

grape seed oil for greasing parchment

1 egg white

1 Tbsp (15 mL) lime juice

1 tsp (5 mL) grape seed oil

Five-spice Mix

2 Tbsp (30 mL) sugar

2 Tbsp (30 mL) Chinese five-spice powder

1 1/2 tsp (7 mL) kosher salt

Curry Spice Mix

2 Tbsp (30 mL) sugar

1 Tbsp (15 mL) curry powder

1 1/2 tsp (7 mL) kosher salt

pinch (or more) of cayenne pepper

2 1/2 cups (625 mL) raw pumpkin seeds (hulls left on)

Preheat oven to 350°F (175°C). Line a rimmed baking sheet with parchment paper, and oil paper lightly.

In a large bowl, whisk together egg white, lime juice and grape seed oil. Whisk in your choice of Five-spice Mix or Curry Spice Mix. Stir in pumpkin seeds to coat thoroughly. Transfer to baking sheet, spreading as much as possible into a single layer—there will be a few clumps, but they can be easily broken apart later.

Bake until toasted, stirring about every 5 minutes (and breaking up clumps), for 20 to 25 minutes. Cool completely on sheet, then transfer to an airtight container.

1 serving (Five-spice Mix): 100 Calories; 5 g Total Fat (1.5 g Mono, 3 g Poly, 1 g Sat); 0 mg Cholesterol; 4g Carbohydrates (0 g Fibre, 2 g Sugar); 4 g Protein; 350 mg Sodium

1 serving (Curry Spice Mix): 100 Calories; 5 g Total Fat (1.5 g Mono, 3 g Poly, 0.5 g Sat); 0 mg Cholesterol; 3 g Carbohydrates (0 g Fibre, 2 g Sugar); 3 g Protein; 350 mg Sodium

Tip

Pumpkin seeds can be stored at room temperature for up to 5 days.

If you think that too much turkey makes you sleepy after a holiday dinner, think again. A recent Ontario study suggests that pumpkin seeds may be the more likely culprit: .03 oz (1 g) pumpkin seed protein has the same amount of tryptophan (an amino acid) as a glass of milk.

Spicy Sunflower Seed Brittle

Serves 14

Sunflowers are a truly native North American species of plant, and aboriginal peoples have cultivated them for thousands of years for food, oil and even dye. Today, sunflowers grow in backyards across Canada, and we continue to be one of the top producers of confectionary sunflowers (those grown for eating rather than for oil) in the world. Our recipe transforms the seeds from savoury snack to sweet, though this candy is definitely for adults. Adjust the heat if you like, by using more or less cayenne. You will need parchment paper, a rolling pin, a candy thermometer, a pastry brush and a pizza cutter for this recipe.

1 1/2 cups (375 mL) raw, hulled sunflower seeds

1/2 tsp (2 mL) cayenne pepper

2 cups (500 mL) sugar

1 cup (250 mL) water

1/4 tsp (1 mL) fine sea salt

This recipe is an easy introduction to making candy. It requires only a few inexpensive specialty items and, if you follow the directions carefully, it will reward you with spectacular and delicious results.

Cover work surface with a 24 x 12 inch (61 x 30 cm) piece of parchment paper and anchor its corners with tape or weights. Cut a second piece of parchment to same dimensions and have ready nearby, along with rolling pin and pizza cutter.

In a medium bowl, mix together sunflower seeds and cayenne.

In a heavy medium saucepan, combine sugar, water and sea salt. Clip candy thermometer to side of pan, making sure bottom is immersed in mixture but not touching bottom of pan. Bring to a boil on medium-high heat, stirring constantly until sugar has dissolved. Once dissolved, do not stir any further.

Continue to cook, washing down any sugar crystals that form on sides of pan with a pastry brush dipped in cold water, until syrup reaches 238°F (114°C) on candy thermometer, about 10 minutes (sugar syrup will still be colourless). Remove from heat and reduce heat to medium. With a wooden spoon, stir in sunflower seeds and cayenne. Continue stirring, off the heat, until syrup crystallizes and becomes gritty, 3 to 4 minutes.

Return pan to heat. Cook, stirring constantly. At first, the sugar will become drier and grainy. Continue to cook until sugar is completely melted and turns a deep caramel colour (about 300°F [150°C] on candy thermometer), 4 to 5 minutes. Remove from heat and carefully pour onto anchored parchment. Cover with second piece of parchment. Pressing firmly with rolling pin, quickly roll out mixture as thinly as possible between pieces of parchment. Remove top sheet of parchment and quickly cut brittle into long strips using the pizza cutter. Allow to cool completely before removing bottom paper.

Once cool, transfer to a parchment-lined airtight container, separating layers of brittle with parchment. Brittle can be stored this way for up to 2 weeks.

1 serving: 200 Calories; 8 g Total Fat (1.5 g Mono, 5 g Poly, 1 g Sat); 0 mg Cholesterol; 32 g Carbohydrates (2 g Fibre, 29 g Sugar) 4 g Protein; 40 mg Sodium

Tip

For a more traditional look, allow brittle to cool completely, then break into pieces of various sizes.

Root Vegetable Chips

Serves 5

There's more to chips than potatoes. The savoury, earthy and slightly sweet flavour of these colourful chips will delight, and former root vegetable haters will quickly change their tune—even kids will eat them up. These chips make a great snack by themselves or with your favourite dip.

3 or 4 large beets

4 large carrots

3 large parsnips

1 medium sweet potato

vegetable oil, as needed

salt to taste

Peel vegetables and use a mandolin or peeler to slice them into very thin rounds or strips. Pat pieces dry with paper towels. You can either deep-fry or bake the chips.

If you have a deep-fryer, follow manufacturer's directions. If not, use a large saucepan to deep-fry on your stove. Put at least 3 inches (7.5 cm) of vegetable oil into saucepan, making sure oil has plenty of headspace. Using a candy thermometer as a gauge, preheat oil to 350°F (175°C). Carefully add vegetable slices in batches, and fry until crisp and golden. Remove with slotted spoon and drain on baking sheet lined with paper towel. Sprinkle lightly with salt—be careful not to sprinkle salt in the oil.

To bake, preheat oven to 225°F (110°C). In a large bowl, toss vegetable strips with 1 to 2 Tbsp (15 to 30 mL) oil and a pinch of salt. Arrange in a single layer on 2 baking sheets. Roast for 1 hour, then rotate trays. Roast 1 more hour until vegetables are crisp and dry, stirring or flipping vegetables occasionally. Keep chips in an airtight container or resealable plastic bag for up to 3 days. To recrisp chips that have gone soft, bake for 10 minutes at 250°F (120°C).

1 serving: 210 Calories; 11 g Total Fat (7 g Mono, 3 g Poly, 1 g Sat); 0 mg Cholesterol; 27 g Carbohydrates; 6 g Fibre; 12 g Sugar; 3 g Protein; 190 mg Sodium

Tip

If you decide to deep-fry, begin with the light-coloured vegetables and end with the dark—the darker ones may colour the oil. If you decide to bake, keep light-coloured vegetables separate from darker ones. Use golden or candy cane beet varieties if you don't want beet juice to stain your hands.

Quick Pickled Autumn Vegetables

Makes 14 cups (3.5 L)

When we feel the first bite of autumn's crisp night air, the race begins to bring in the last of the garden's bounty. Pickles are a great way to preserve your harvest. Our easy refrigerator version warms up the flavours of autumn vegetables with the addition of fresh ginger. These pickles take very little time to make and require no special canning equipment. The best part is that you need not wait long before cracking open your first jar. The pickles taste best after at least 48 hours, but if you absolutely can't resist, go ahead and indulge right away.

1 lb (454 g) beets (halved if small; cut into pieces if larger)

1 lb (454 g) carrots (left whole if small; cut into pieces if larger)

1 lb (454 g) cauliflower, separated into florets

1 lb (454 g) pearl onions, peeled (see Tip, p. 122)

1 1/2 cups (375 mL) rice wine vinegar

1 cup (250 mL) white wine vinegar

1 cup (250 mL) water

2 Tbsp (30 mL) coarse sea salt

2 Tbsp (30 mL) sugar

6 cloves garlic, coarsely chopped

2 Tbsp (30 mL) grated ginger root

1 Tbsp (15 mL) whole coriander

6 whole black peppercorns

Cook each type of vegetable separately until just tender-crisp (leave carrots raw if you prefer). Refresh in ice water. Transfer to sterilized jars (or other non-reactive containers with tight-fitting lids), filling no more than three-quarters full.

Combine vinegars, water, salt, sugar, garlic, ginger and spices in large saucepan over medium-high heat. Bring to a boil, stirring occasionally. Once sugar has dissolved, pour hot pickling liquid over vegetables in jars, leaving 1/2 inch (12 mm) headspace. Screw lids on tightly. Cool to room temperature before transferring to fridge. Pickles will keep up to 2 weeks in the fridge.

1/4 cup (60 mL): 60 Calories; 0 g Total Fat (0 g Mono, 0 g Poly, 0 g Sat); 0 mg Cholesterol; 14 g Carbohydrates (2 g Fibre, 7 g Sugar); 2 g Protein; 290 mg Sodium

Tip

Vegetables may be canned separately or mixed together, though the beets will colour the other vegetables if you combine them.

Smoked Salmon "Tartare" on Corn Cakes

Serves 8

Sweet corn in crisp cakes is a natural complement to the richness of smoked salmon. The corn cakes are especially versatile—in addition to their mini form here as an appetizer, they make a great breakfast when cooked in slightly larger cakes, with or without the smoked salmon. For the tartare, make sure you use a moist smoked salmon, such as lox, pre-sliced or not.

8 oz (225 g) smoked salmon, finely chopped

1/4 cup (60 mL) finely diced yellow pepper

1/4 cup (60 mL) finely chopped red onion

3 Tbsp (45 mL) chopped chives

2 Tbsp (30 mL) lemon juice

1/4 tsp (1 mL) *each* salt and freshly ground pepper

32 corn cakes (see opposite)

2 cups Homemade Crème Fraîche (see p. 53)

Mix first 6 ingredients together in a medium bowl.

To assemble, spread 1 Tbsp (15 mL) crème fraîche on each corn cake. Top with 2 Tbsp (30 mL) salmon mixture, and serve.

1 serving: 260 Calories; 11 g Total Fat (3 g Mono, 4.5 g Poly, 2.5 g Sat); 45 mg Cholesterol; 30 g Carbohydrates (1 g Fibre; 3 g Sugar); 9 g Protein; 810 mg Sodium

Corn Cakes

Makes 32

In a medium bowl, stir together cornmeal, flour, baking soda, sugar, salt, pepper and cayenne. In a large bowl, combine buttermilk, egg and butter, and stir in corn, green onion and both peppers. Add cornmeal mixture and stir until just combined.

Heat large sauté pan on medium-high. Lightly grease with oil. Drop batter in pan, 2 Tbsp (30 mL) at a time, spreading slightly to form 2 1/2 to 3 inch (6 to 7.5 cm) cakes. Cook 2 to 3 minutes per side, until golden and crisp. Transfer to a wire rack to cool.

1 cake: 220 Calorie; 4 g Total Fat (2 g Mono, 4 g Poly, 2.5 g Sat); 40 mg Cholesterol; 29 g Carbohydrates (4 g Fibre, 2 g Sugar); 4 g Protein; 490 mg Sodium

1 cup (250 mL) coarsely ground yellow cornmeal

1/2 cup (125 mL) all-purpose flour

3/4 tsp (4 mL) baking soda

2 tsp (10 mL) sugar

1 tsp (5 mL) salt

1/2 tsp (2 mL) freshly ground pepper

1/4 tsp (1 mL) cayenne pepper

1 cup (250 mL) buttermilk

1 egg

2 Tbsp (30 mL) melted butter, cooled

1 cup (250 mL) coarsely chopped frozen corn, thawed

1/4 cup (60 mL) finely chopped green onion

1/4 cup (60 mL) finely chopped roasted red pepper (see p. 33)

1 small fresh chili pepper, seeded and finely chopped (see Introduction)

grape seed oil, as needed

Wild Mushroom Crostini with Port Reduction

Serves 12

The cool, damp air of autumn mornings provides the ideal climate for a huge variety of wild mushrooms to grow and ripen. A mushroom-picking foray is the perfect excuse to spend an afternoon wandering the woods, but take an educated guide with you because many varieties are toxic and some bear a remarkable resemblance to edible types. An abundance of your favourite varieties will be available at farmers' markets and specialty grocers at this time of year as well. This simple recipe highlights the mushrooms' flavour to the fullest.

2 Tbsp (30 mL) grape seed oil

2 medium shallots, minced

6 cups (1.5 L) wild mushrooms, sliced thinly or pulled into strips

1/2 tsp (2 mL) *each* salt and freshly ground pepper

3/4 cup (175 mL) port wine, *divided*

1/4 cup (60 mL) whipping cream (30 percent)

2 Tbsp (30 mL) chopped fresh thyme

3 oz (95 g) soft goat cheese

6 pieces of crusty bread, cut in half and toasted

sprigs of thyme for garnish

Heat oil in a large sauté pan over medium-low. Add shallots. Cook, stirring, until softened, 1 to 2 minutes. Increase heat to medium. Add mushrooms, and season with salt and pepper. Cook, stirring, about 5 minutes. Add 1/4 cup (60 mL) port. Cook until liquid is absorbed. Add cream and thyme. Continue cooking until mixture is nearly dry.

For the port reduction, simmer remaining 1/2 cup (125 mL) port until reduced by half and slightly thickened, about 5 minutes.

Pile mushrooms on top of toasts. Crumble goat cheese over top. Drizzle with port reduction and garnish with thyme sprigs.

1 serving: 100 Calories; 6 g Total Fat (1.5 g Mono, 2 g Poly, 2.5 g Sat); 10 mg Cholesterol; 9 g Carbohydrates (trace Fibre, 0 g Sugar); 4 g Protein; 190 mg Sodium

Related to onions, shallots are favoured for their milder flavour. Shallots are cooked like onions, but they more closely resemble garlic in their appearance. Shallots grow bulbs with multiple cloves, each separated by a papery skin. Fresh green shallots can be purchased seasonally, but dry shallots are more commonly available.

Cider-roasted Oysters

Serves 8

Oysters are a pleasure to eat raw on the half shell or cooked on the grill. This recipe is a perfect showcase for larger varieties of oyster and is an excellent way to introduce a novice to the wonderful world of these succulent, sweet, briny treats. Cooking the oysters this way infuses the flavours of the sauce all the way through the meat.

1 Tbsp (15 mL) butter

3 Tbsp (45 mL) minced shallots

3/4 cup (175 mL) apple or pear cider

2 Tbsp (30 mL) grainy Dijon mustard

1 Tbsp (15 mL) chopped fresh thyme

1 tsp (5 mL) chopped capers

salt and freshly ground pepper to taste

24 fresh oysters in the shell

Preheat grill to medium-high. Melt butter in small saucepan over medium-low heat. Stir in shallots and cook about 1 minute, until fragrant. Pour cider into pan and cook until slightly reduced, about 10 minutes. Remove from heat and stir in mustard, thyme and capers to blend. Season with salt and pepper. Set aside.

Remove oysters from their shells (see Tip) and rinse oysters and shells separately under cold running water. Drain well. Place each oyster in a cupped half shell and spoon sauce overtop. Put oyster shells directly on grill and cook 3 to 5 minutes until edges of oysters start to curl (see Tip).

1 serving: 160 Calories; 4.5 g Total Fat (1 g Mono, 1.5 g Poly, 1.5 g Sat); 90 mg Cholesterol; 13 g Carbohydrates (0 g Fibre, 3 g Sugar); 15 g Protein; 270 mg Sodium

Tip

To fast-track these oysters, just pop the unshucked shells straight onto the grill to steam open (oysters that do not open should be discarded), then remove the flat shell and spoon sauce onto each oyster just before serving.

Tip

Always buy oysters alive and fresh. The shell should be tightly closed, or, if slightly open, should close promptly when tapped. If the shell is open and does not close when tapped, or it is broken, throw the oyster out. Store oysters refrigerated on ice and covered with a damp cloth.

To shuck oysters, first scrub shells with a stiff-bristled brush. With a towel folded in the palm of your hand, hold shell firmly with cupped side facing down. Use an oyster knife to pry shell open and detach the top shell. Scrape oyster from the bottom shell. (Your fishmonger will shuck the oysters if you're going to eat them the same day.)

Beet Carpaccio with Arugula Pesto

Serves 6

Beef carpaccio is the classic dish named after Venetian painter Vittore Carpaccio, who favoured bright, dark reds in his paintings. Here, beets, long an autumn and winter staple, lend their bright colours and earthy flavour to the dish. Look for chioggia (also known as candy cane), purple and golden beets at your local farmers' markets; they have a sweeter, more mellow flavour than darker varieties and won't stain your hands or work surfaces.

12 x 2 inch (5 cm) beets, trimmed (use any combination)

1/4 cup (60 mL) extra virgin olive oil

salt and freshly ground pepper to taste

8 oz (225 g) crumbled soft, fresh goat cheese

1/2 cup (125 mL) Arugula Pesto (see opposite)

Preheat oven to 350°F (175°C). Line a rimmed baking sheet with foil. Place beets on sheet (if you are using more than one kind of beet, cook them separately in pie plates). Sprinkle beets lightly with water. Cover tightly with foil. Bake until beets are tender, about 40 minutes. Cool, peel and slice beets very thinly with a mandolin or cheese slicer.

In a medium bowl, combine olive oil, salt and pepper. Toss each type of beet separately in olive oil mixture, beginning with the lightest-coloured beets and ending with the darkest. Arrange slices on 6 plates, dividing equally. Sprinkle with goat cheese. Drizzle pesto over top.

1 serving: 360 Calories; 28 g Total Fat (15 g Mono, 3.5 g Poly, 9 g Sat); 25 mg Cholesterol; 17 g Carbohydrates (3 g Fibre, 12 g Sugar); 13 g Protein; 420 mg Sodium

Tip
Beets can be prepared a day ahead.

Arugula Pesto

Makes about 2 cups (500 mL)

While beets are cooking, pulse arugula and garlic in a blender until well crushed. Add nuts, process to crush, then add cheese. You should have a thick paste. Slowly drizzle in olive oil, continuously mixing. Season to taste with salt and pepper. Store in the fridge with a thin layer of olive oil or piece of plastic wrap directly on top for up to 2 weeks.

1/4 cup (60 mL): 560 Calories; 59 g Total Fat (38 g Mono, 9 g Poly, 10 g Sat); 15 mg Cholesterol; 4 g Carbohydrates (trace Fibre, trace Sugar); 10 g Protein; 330 mg Sodium

4 packed cups (1 L) fresh arugula leaves, rinsed and patted dry

4 cloves garlic

1 cup (250 mL) pine nuts (or other nuts of your choice)

1 1/2 cups (375 mL) freshly grated Parmesan or pecorino cheese

1 1/2 cups (375 mL) extra virgin olive oil

salt and freshly ground pepper to taste

Gingered Squash Soup

Serves 6

What better way to enjoy autumn's abundant harvest than with a bowl of steaming hot soup? There are so many combinations and possibilities, you could make a new soup every day and still never try them all. In this creamy puréed soup, apple and ginger add undercurrents of sweetness and heat to make the flavour of butternut squash sing.

2 butternut squash, cut in half lengthwise, seeded

2 Tbsp (30 mL) grape seed oil

2 cups (500 mL) chopped yellow onion

1 medium Gala apple, peeled, cored and chopped

2 cloves garlic, minced

2 Tbsp (30 mL) minced ginger root

1 Tbsp (15 mL) brown sugar

1/2 cinnamon stick

4 cups (1 L) chicken broth

1 cup (250 mL) whipping cream (30 percent) plus more for garnish

salt and freshly ground pepper to taste

fresh chives for garnish

Preheat oven to 375°F (190°C). Lightly oil a baking sheet with grape seed oil. Place squash cut side down on baking sheet. Bake until very tender, about 50 minutes. Use a paring knife to cut peel from squash. Discard peel. Cut squash into 2 inch (5 cm) pieces.

Heat oil in a large saucepan over medium-low. Add onion, apple, garlic, ginger, sugar and cinnamon. Cook, stirring, until onion and apple are softened and golden, about 15 minutes. Add squash and chicken broth. Bring to a boil over medium-high heat. Reduce heat to medium-low. Cover and simmer 10 minutes. Discard cinnamon stick.

Purée soup with a hand blender or in batches in a blender. Return to heat. Stir in cream. Season with salt and pepper. Bring to a simmer. Remove from heat and ladle into bowls to serve. Garnish with drops of cream and chives.

1 serving: 300 Calories; 18 g Total Fat (4.5 g Mono, 4 g Poly, 8 g Sat); 454 mg Cholesterol; 49 g Carbohydrates (5 g Fibre, 13 g Sugar); 6 g Protein; 570 mg Sodium

The combination of corn, beans and squash is referred to as the Three Sisters because they are companion plants. First Nations people all over the Americas planted corn and beans in mounds so the tall corn stalks would provide support for the climbing beans, and squash around the mounds, where the large leaves shaded the soil and prevented weed growth. Now we have another reason to associate the three vegetables: when eaten together, they form a complete protein for a meatless meal.

Chestnut Fennel Soup

Serves 4

When settlers first arrived in the forests of southern Ontario, American chestnut trees were a common sight and one of the most abundant food sources in the area. Settlers boiled, roasted and candied the nuts, and ground them into flour to use in baking. Most of these trees succumbed to blight in the early 1900s, but there is hope that they will make a comeback. In the tree's natural regions, Ontario has the largest number of trees that proved resistant to the blight anywhere, and Nova Scotia has one of the largest trees still standing.

2 cups (500 mL) roasted, shelled and skinned chestnuts (about 1 lb, 454 g, in shell; see p. 67)

1 shallot, minced

2 leeks (white and pale green parts only), coarsely chopped

6 Tbsp (90 mL) unsalted butter, *divided*

1/4 cup (60 mL) dry white wine

3 cups (750 mL) chicken broth

1/2 fennel bulb (stalks and core discarded), coarsely chopped

1 Tbsp (15 mL) toasted, ground fennel seeds

1 Tbsp (15 mL) grated nutmeg

1 tsp (5 mL) ground allspice

1/2 cup (125 mL) light cream (18 percent)

sea salt and freshly ground pepper to taste

Coarsely chop chestnuts, reserving 1/3 cup (75 mL) for garnish. Set aside.

Cook shallot and leeks in 2 Tbsp (30 mL) butter in a large saucepan over medium heat, stirring occasionally, until softened. Add wine. Simmer until liquid has nearly all evaporated, about 1 minute. Stir in broth, chopped chestnuts (excluding garnish), chopped fennel bulb, fennel seeds, nutmeg and allspice. Simmer, uncovered, 30 minutes. Stir in cream and remove from heat.

Purée soup with hand blender until smooth. Return to heat and bring to a simmer. Season with salt and pepper.

While soup is reheating, heat remaining 4 Tbsp (60 mL) butter in a medium sauté pan over medium-high until foam subsides, then sauté reserved chestnuts with salt and pepper, stirring constantly, until crisp and butter is browned, about 4 minutes.

Divide soup among serving bowls, top with reserved chestnuts and drizzle with brown butter.

1 serving: 460 Calories; 25 g Total Fat (7 g Mono, 1.5 g Poly, 15 g Sat); 65 mg Cholesterol; 52 g Carbohydrates (7 g Fibre, 11 g Sugar); 7 g Protein; 810 mg Sodium

Tip

You can substitute 14 oz (398 mL) canned whole chestnuts or 14 oz (398 mL) of chestnut purée for fresh roasted chestnuts, but if you use the purée, you'll still need a few whole chestnuts (canned or fresh) for the garnish.

Curried Carrot and Parsnip Soup

Serves 4

Autumn's bounty of sweet carrots and lightly perfumed parsnips are at their best here, puréed into a silky soup and given a touch of the exotic with curry, coconut and lime. Once considered almost interchangeable, carrots have long eclipsed their cousin's popularity, but given a chance, parsnips are sure to impress with their delicate, aromatic flavour. Besides, despite their pale colour, parsnips are actually richer in vitamins and minerals than carrots; they're a great source of vitamin C, potassium, folic acid and fibre. Like beets, parsnips develop their full flavour after a frost, so this soup is made for frosty late autumn days.

5 large carrots, peeled and chopped

5 parsnips, peeled and chopped

1 Tbsp (15 mL) grape seed oil

1 medium white or yellow onion, diced

1 thumb-sized knob of ginger, peeled and minced

3 to 5 bird chilies, seeded and minced (see Introduction)

2 tsp (10 mL) curry powder (or more to taste)

pinch of nutmeg

1 head of garlic, roasted (see Tip) and cloves squeezed out

(see next page)

In a large pan, sauté carrots and parsnips in grape seed oil over medium-high heat until they start to colour a little. Reduce heat to medium-low and add onion, ginger, bird chilies, curry powder and nutmeg. Sauté until onions soften, about 5 minutes. Add roasted garlic cloves and broth, and simmer about 10 minutes.

Purée with a hand blender (or in batches in a blender) until smooth. Add coconut milk and lime juice; bring to a simmer. Thin to desired consistency with additional broth or coconut milk. Season with salt and pepper. Serve in bowls with a dollop of yogurt and a sprinkle of chopped cilantro and nuts on top.

1 serving: 460 Calories; 23 g Total Fat (2 g Mono, 3 g Poly, 16 g Sat); 0 mg Cholesterol; 63 g Carbohydrates (14 g Fibre, 20 g Sugar); 11 g Protein; 1070 mg Sodium

Tip

To roast garlic, preheat oven to 350°F (175°C), though if you'd like to do this while baking something else, you could do it in an oven anywhere from 325 to 375°F (160 to 190°C) and adjust the cooking time. Cut the top off a head of garlic (which will make it easier to squeeze the cloves out once they're cooked), then rub it all over with a little grape seed oil. Wrap in foil and set in a pie plate. If you have a clay garlic roaster, skip the foil. Roast for about 1 hour, until very soft. To use, squeeze the cloves from the peels. We recommend roasting more than you need for any given recipe, as you'll find many uses for it (it's delicious just spread on toast). Store in the fridge for up to 2 weeks.

5 cups (1.25 L) chicken or vegetable broth

1 1/2 cups (375 mL) coconut milk

juice of 1 lime

salt and freshly ground pepper to taste

plain yogurt for garnish

1 bunch of fresh cilantro, chopped

chopped peanuts or cashews for garnish

Corn and Smoked Salmon Chowder with Pistou

Serves 7

Hot-smoked salmon (often sold as "BBQ tips") brings a smoky flavour to this rich, hearty chowder. Cooking the stripped corn cobs in the broth helps thicken the soup and ensures that you get as much sweet corn flavour as possible. This soup keeps well in the fridge for a couple days, improving in flavour; leftovers make a quick and satisfying lunch with a hunk of crusty sourdough to mop out the bowl. Pistou is a pesto-like accompaniment to soups and pastas.

6 ears of corn, shucked

10 cups (2.5 L) Homemade Fish Stock (see p. 57) or Homemade Chicken Stock (see p. 37)

2 Tbsp (30 mL) grape seed oil

2 leeks (white and pale green parts only), washed well and chopped fine

1 large sweet onion, diced into 1/2 inch (12 mm) pieces

1 large baking potato (about 1/2 lb, 225 g), peeled and diced into 1/2 inch (12 mm) pieces

1 bay leaf

1/2 tsp (2 mL) dried thyme

salt and freshly ground pepper to taste

1 lb (454 g) smoked salmon (not lox), chopped

1 1/2 cup (375 mL) light cream (18 percent)

1 red bell pepper, roasted (see Tip) and chopped fine

Pistou (see opposite)

Cut corn kernels from cobs and set kernels aside. Break cobs in half. Bring broth to a boil in a large saucepan over medium heat. Add corn cobs, cover and simmer about 20 minutes. Pull out cobs with tongs and discard. Transfer broth to a large bowl.

Heat oil in a saucepan over medium-low. Add leeks and onion, and cook, stirring, until softened, about 5 minutes. Add potato, bay leaf, thyme and a pinch each of salt and pepper, and cook, stirring, another 10 minutes. Add corn kernels and broth. Simmer, uncovered, for 10 minutes. Remove 2 cups (500 mL) of chowder and purée with a hand blender (or in a blender). Return puréed chowder to saucepan. Stir in smoked salmon, cream and roasted pepper. Heat over medium, stirring, until hot, but be careful not to let it boil. Taste and adjust seasoning. Ladle into bowls and top each serving with a dollop of pistou.

1 serving: 530 Calories; 34 g Total Fat (17 g Mono, 6 g Poly, 10 g Sat); 50 mg Cholesterol; 37 g Carbohydrates (6 g Fibre, 7 g Sugar); 24 g Protein; 1420 mg Sodium

Pistou

Makes 1 cup (250 mL)

In a food processor, purée basil, Parmesan and garlic. Slowly drizzle in oil and season with salt and pepper. Blend until smooth. Stir pistou into soups or toss it with cooked pasta or vegetables. Pistou will keep, chilled, in an airtight container for up to 1 week.

3 Tbsp (45 mL): 170 Calories; 17 g Total Fat (12 g Mono, 2 g Poly, 3 g Sat); trace Cholesterol; 3 g Carbohydrates (2 g Fibre, 0 g Sugar); 3 g Protein; 100 mg Sodium

Tip

Roast peppers over a live flame, such as a gas burner or a gas or charcoal grill, or on the highest rack of the oven under a broiler. Preheat your selected heat source on high (500°F, 260°C, for a broiler). Coat the peppers lightly with grape seed oil. Watching carefully, place peppers over or under the heat source. Turn peppers gradually as the skin begins to blister and blacken, until the peppers are blackened all over, up to 20 minutes in total depending on the heat source. Transfer to a bowl and cover with plastic wrap. Set aside about 20 minutes. Slide or rub off the skins, then pull out the seeds and pulp. Cut open and lay flat, then use a knife to scrape out remaining seeds or ribs.

8 packed cups (2 L) fresh basil leaves, rinsed and spun dry

1/4 cup (60 mL) freshly grated Parmesan cheese

2 cloves garlic, minced

1/2 cup (125 mL) olive oil

salt and freshly ground pepper to taste

Roasted Vegetable Soup

Serves 6

This soup is perfect for those days when the calendar says autumn but it already feels like winter. Roasting brings out the full flavours of the vegetables and will fill your kitchen with delicious aromas before the soup even goes on the stove. This soup freezes exceptionally well, so make a double batch and put some away for a quick meal on a cold winter day.

3 medium carrots, peeled and quartered lengthwise

1 large onion, cut into 8 wedges

1/2 small butternut squash, peeled, seeded, cut lengthwise into 1/2 inch (12 mm) thick wedges

1 to 2 Tbsp (15 to 30 mL) olive oil

1 Tbsp (15 mL) chopped fresh thyme

salt and freshly ground pepper to taste

1 head of garlic, unpeeled

4 to 6 Roma tomatoes, halved

6 cups (1.5 L) Homemade Vegetable Stock (see p. 77), divided

4 cups (1 L) finely chopped kale

1/2 cup (125 mL) dried beans, soaked overnight (see Tip)

3 sprigs of fresh thyme

1 Tbsp (15 mL) marjoram

1 bay leaf

1/2 tsp (2 mL) cayenne pepper

crusty bread

Preheat oven to 400°F (200°C). In a large bowl, toss carrots, onion and squash with oil, thyme, salt and pepper. Arrange in a single layer on a heavy, rimmed baking pan. Rub head of garlic with a little olive oil and place in corner of baking pan. Toss tomatoes in same bowl to coat, and arrange in a single layer on a second baking pan, so their juices don't make the other vegetables steam instead of roast. Cook until vegetables are tender and golden, stirring occasionally, about 45 minutes.

Transfer carrots and squash to work surface. Cut into 1/2 inch (12 mm) pieces; set aside. Squeeze garlic cloves from peels into a food processor or blender. Add tomatoes and onion; purée until almost smooth.

Pour 1/2 cup (125 mL) stock into first baking pan; scrape up any browned bits. Repeat with second baking pan. Transfer stock and vegetable purée to a large pot. Add remaining stock, kale, beans, thyme, marjoram, bay leaf and cayenne. Bring to a boil. Reduce heat and simmer, uncovered, until kale and beans are tender, about 30 minutes.

Everyone knows that some soups are better the next day, and that's especially true of this one. Just bring it back up to a simmer before serving.

Add reserved carrots and squash to soup. Simmer about 10 minutes to blend flavours, thinning soup with additional stock if necessary. Season with salt and pepper. Remove and discard thyme sprigs and bay leaf. Serve with crusty bread.

1 serving: 170 Calories; 3 g Total Fat (1.5 g Mono, 0.5 g Poly, 0 g Sat); 0 mg Cholesterol; 33 g Carbohydrates (7 g Fibre; 8 g Sugar); 7 g Protein; 670 mg Sodium

Tip

Try orca, cranberry or scarlet runner beans in this recipe. If you forget to soak your beans the night before, just simmer in water for 1 1/2 hours before adding them to the recipe.

Chicken Soup with Orzo and Autumn Greens

Serves 4

Yes, this is a recipe for a slightly more nutritious version of that old childhood favourite, chicken noodle soup. And what could be more warming or more comforting on a chilly autumn day? You might be tempted to take a shortcut and make this recipe with a commercially prepared chicken broth—don't. A good, homemade, full-bodied chicken (or turkey) stock is absolutely essential to this recipe. Trust us, your tastebuds and your soul will thank you.

1 Tbsp (15 mL) grape seed oil

2 Tbsp (30 mL) minced garlic

2 Tbsp (30 mL) minced shallots

6 cups (1.5 L) Homemade Chicken Stock (see opposite)

3/4 cup (175 mL) uncooked orzo

1 bunch of rainbow chard, (sorrel or kale) cut crosswise into 1/2 inch (12 mm) wide strips

1 lb (454 g) boneless skinless chicken breast, cut into 1 inch (2.5 cm) pieces

salt and freshly ground pepper to taste

Heat oil in a large saucepan over medium-low. Add garlic and shallots. Cook, stirring, until softened, about 1 minute. Add chicken stock. Bring to a boil over medium-high. Stir in orzo. Reduce heat to medium. Simmer until orzo is slightly undercooked, about 6 minutes. Stir in chard and chicken, and simmer until chicken is cooked through, about 5 minutes. Season with salt and pepper. Ladle into bowls and serve immediately.

1 serving: 330 Calories; 5 g Total Fat (1 g Mono, 3 g Poly, 0.5 g Sat); 65 mg Cholesterol; 34 g Carbohydrates (4 g Fibre, 5 g Sugar) 35 g Protein; 1500 mg Sodium

Tip

Our homemade chicken stock could be used instead of the chicken broth called for in other recipes in this book. It is cooked in the oven instead of on the stovetop because the oven provides a more gentle, even heat. Cooking for a longer time allows more flavour to develop.

Homemade Chicken Stock

Makes 12 cups (3 L)

Preheat oven to 180°F (82°C). Place chicken bones
in a large, ovenproof saucepan. Add water and bring to
a boil over medium-high heat. Skim foam that rises to the
surface. Cover. Transfer saucepan to oven. Cook 3 to
5 hours, skimming occasionally and checking to make sure
it's not bubbling (it shouldn't bubble, but should be hot to
the touch).

Add celery, carrots, onions, garlic, parsley, thyme, bay leaf
and peppercorns. Cook 1 more hour.

Remove from oven. Strain through colander. Discard solids.
Strain again through cheesecloth-lined sieve. Discard
solids. If using immediately, skim fat from surface and
discard. If not, cool, uncovered, to room temperature, then
chill, covered, until fat solidifies. Skim off and discard fat.
Keep covered in refrigerator for up to 3 days, or freeze for
up to 3 months.

*1 cup (250 mL): 10 Calories; 0 g Total Fat (0 g Mono, 0 g Poly,
0 g Sat); trace Cholesterol; 1 g Carbohydrates (0 g Fibre,
0 g Sugar); 1 g Protein; 10 mg Sodium*

**3 to 4 lbs (1.4 to 1.8 kg)
chicken bones**

16 cups (4 L) cold water

**2 celery ribs, cut into
2 inch (5 cm) pieces**

**2 carrots, cut into 2 inch
(5 cm) pieces**

**2 medium onions,
unpeeled, quartered**

4 cloves garlic, crushed

6 stems of fresh parsley

2 sprigs of fresh thyme

1 bay leaf

8 whole black peppercorns

Apple, Fennel and Celeriac Salad with Cider Vinaigrette

Serves 4

Celeriac, or celery root, is not the root of just any celery plant—it's the root from a special variety of celery. Its gnarled, hairy exterior belies the delicate flavour of its flesh, which tastes somewhat like a cross between celery and jicama and has the crispness of celery without the stringy fibres. Celeriac can be boiled, roasted or eaten raw, as in this salad.

1 large fennel bulb

1 Tbsp (15 mL) lemon juice

2 cups (500 mL) cold water

1/2 small celeriac, peeled (see Tip)

3 crisp sweet apples, such as Gala or Fuji, halved and cored

1 cup (250 mL) unfiltered apple cider

3 Tbsp (45 mL) minced shallots

2 Tbsp (30 mL) cider vinegar

2 tsp (10 mL) grainy mustard

1/4 tsp (1 mL) *each* salt and freshly ground pepper

1/3 cup (75 mL) extra virgin olive oil

Trim outer leaves and bottom of fennel bulb, leaving core attached. Cut in half, then use a knife or mandolin to slice each half lengthwise into paper-thin slices. Set aside. In a medium bowl, mix lemon juice with cold water. Cut celeriac in half and slice each piece crosswise into paper-thin slices. Transfer slices immediately to bowl of acidulated water to keep them from turning brown. Cut apples into paper-thin slices and transfer to acidulated water.

For the vinaigrette, bring cider to a boil in a small saucepan. Simmer 12 to 15 minutes, until reduced to about 1/3 cup (75 mL).

Acidulated water will keep certain fruits and vegetables from turning brown. In this recipe, the acidulated water is made from water and lemon juice.

In a small bowl, combine reduced cider, shallots, vinegar, mustard, salt and pepper. Mix well. Slowly drizzle in oil while whisking vigorously, until well combined.

To assemble, drain celeriac and apple slices in a colander, then use paper towel to soak up any remaining water. Place in a large bowl with fennel slices. Drizzle cider vinaigrette over and toss. Divide among 4 plates.

1 serving: 350 Calories; 19 g Total Fat (15 g Mono, 1.5 g Poly, 3 g Sat); 0 mg Cholesterol; 48 g Carbohydrates (7 g Fibre, 26 g Sugar); 3 g Protein; 290 mg Sodium

Tip

Use a knife rather than a peeler to take the skin off the celeriac—the skin is too rough and bumpy for a peeler. You'll lose some of the flesh, but save yourself some frustration.

Endive, Pear and Walnut Salad with Rosemary Vinaigrette

Serves 4

Autumn just wouldn't be the same without the pear. Green ones, red ones, golden ones, the rounded curves of the Bartlett, the elongated form of the Bosc—the pear's beauty has been celebrated by artists in their still-lifes for centuries. In this autumn salad, we celebrate its flavour and crisp, juicy texture by pairing it with salty Parmigiano-Reggiano cheese, rich toasted walnuts and an herby rosemary dressing.

1 head curly endive

2 tsp (10 mL) lemon juice

1 cup (250 mL) cold water

2 firm ripe pears

2 Tbsp (30 mL) pear vinegar or white wine vinegar

2 Tbsp (30 mL) chopped fresh rosemary

1 1/2 Tbsp (22 mL) minced shallots

1 Tbsp (15 mL) chopped fresh parsley

1/4 tsp (1 mL) *each* salt and freshly ground pepper

1/3 cup (75 mL) extra virgin olive oil

1/4 cup (60 mL) coarsely chopped toasted walnuts

1/4 cup (60 mL) shaved Parmiggiano-Reggiano

1/4 cup (60 mL) pomegranate seeds

Wash and chop endive. Set aside. Combine lemon juice with cold water. Halve and core pears. With a knife or mandolin cut pear halves lengthwise into paper-thin slices and transfer immediately to acidulated water.

For the vinaigrette, combine vinegar, rosemary, shallots, parsley, salt and pepper in a small bowl. Purée with a hand blender while drizzling in oil, until well combined.

Drain pear slices in a colander, then use paper towel to soak up any remaining water. Combine in a large bowl with endive. Drizzle vinaigrette over and toss. Divide among 4 plates. Sprinkle walnuts, Parmiggiano-Reggiano and pomegranate seeds over top.

1 serving: 320 Calories: 26 g Total Fat (16 g Mono, 5 g Poly, 4.5 g Sat); 5 mg Cholesterol; 23 g Carbohydrate (7 g Fibre, 12 g Sugar); 6 g Protein; 270 mg Sodium

 *Parmigiano-Reggiano is Parmesan produced in Italy. It is certified as being of the highest quality, with a complex flavour that is often absent from generic varieties.*

Seven Grain Salad with Maple Balsamic Vinaigrette

Serves 8

If you're looking for a way to incorporate more whole grains into your diet, we've got a delicious suggestion for you. This mixed grain salad is a great starter or side dish but also makes a great, easy-to-pack lunch. Technically, quinoa is a seed, but it is cooked as a grain in many recipes.

1/2 cup (125 mL) black rice

1/2 cup (125 mL) brown rice

1/2 cup (125 mL) pearl barley

1/2 cup (125 mL) wild rice

1/2 cup (125 mL) wheatberries

6 cups (1.5 L) water, *divided*

1/2 cup (125 mL) millet

1/2 cup (125 mL) quinoa

1/3 cup (75 mL) extra virgin olive oil

2 Tbsp (30 mL) balsamic vinegar

1 Tbsp (15 mL) chopped fresh parsley

1 Tbsp (15 mL) maple syrup

1 tsp (5 mL) lemon zest

salt and freshly ground pepper to taste

(see next page)

Combine black rice, brown rice, pearl barley, wild rice and wheat berries in medium saucepan with 3 1/2 cups (875 mL) water. Bring to a boil over medium-high heat. Stir, then reduce heat to low. Cover and cook until grains are tender and liquid is absorbed, about 40 minutes. Remove from heat and let cool.

Meanwhile, combine millet and quinoa in second medium saucepan with 2 1/2 cups (625 mL) water. Bring to a boil over medium-high heat. Stir. Reduce heat to low. Cover and cook until grains are tender and liquid is absorbed, about 15 minutes. Remove from heat and let cool.

In a small bowl, use a hand blender or whisk to combine olive oil, vinegar, parsley, maple syrup, lemon zest, salt and pepper.

In a large bowl, combine grains, artichoke hearts, onions, peppers, tomatoes, basil and vinaigrette. Toss well. Serve at room temperature. Keep leftovers covered in the refrigerator for up to 3 days.

1 serving: 440 Calories; 18 g Total Fat (11 g Mono, 1.5 g Poly, 2.5 g Sat); 0 mg Cholesterol; 65 g Carbohydrate (8 g Fibre, 7 g Sugar); 9 g Protein; 150 mg Sodium

Tip

You can replace any of the grains in this recipe with other types of grain. Just watch out for cooking times. Or, make this recipe even easier by using a commercially packaged multi-grain blend.

3 to 4 marinated artichoke hearts, sliced

1/2 cup (125 mL) chopped red onion

1/2 cup (125 mL) chopped roasted yellow pepper (see p. 33)

4 Roma tomatoes, cut into wedges

1/4 cup (60 mL) fresh basil, thinly sliced

Brussels Sprout Leaf Salad with Bacon Vinaigrette

Serves 7

Brussels sprouts can be so much more than the tiny under- or over-cooked cabbages that we are forced to eat once or twice a year as part of a traditional holiday meal. Separated into individual leaves, the much-maligned Brussels sprout takes on a whole new character in this warm salad. The bacon vinaigrette is sure to win praises.

1 1/2 lbs (680 g) Brussels sprouts

5 slices bacon, cut into 1/2 inch (12 mm) strips

1/2 cup (125 mL) finely chopped apple

2 Tbsp (30 mL) minced shallots

1 1/2 cups (375 mL) apple cider

2 Tbsp (30 mL) cider vinegar

1/4 tsp (1 mL) salt

1 tsp (5 mL) freshly ground black pepper

1 Tbsp (15 mL) chopped fresh thyme

1 tsp (5 mL) Dijon mustard

1 Tbsp (15 mL) extra virgin olive oil

Rinse Brussels sprouts. Remove and discard any discoloured leaves. Use a sharp paring knife to trim stem end of each sprout, releasing a layer of leaves, then pull the leaves from the sprout and drop into a large bowl. Continue stripping leaves from the sprout until only about 1/2 inch (12 mm) remains of centre of sprout; cut this piece in half lengthwise. Repeat with remaining sprouts.

In a large sauté pan, cook bacon over medium-high heat until crisp, stirring often to prevent burning, about 10 minutes. Transfer with slotted spoon to paper towels to drain. Set aside. Pour all but 2 Tbsp (30 mL) bacon drippings from pan into separate container and set aside.

Reduce heat to medium. Add apple and shallots to pan. Cook, stirring, until slightly softened, about 1 minute. Add cider, vinegar, salt and pepper. Bring to a boil and cook, stirring occasionally, until reduced to about 1/2 cup (125 mL), 8 to 10 minutes. Remove from heat.

In a small bowl, stir together thyme and mustard. Whisk in cider reduction, then oil.

Add 1 Tbsp (15 mL) reserved bacon drippings to pan (discard remaining drippings). Heat over medium-high. Add Brussels sprout leaves and centres. Cook, stirring, until just wilted, 3 to 4 minutes. Add bacon and dressing. Stir until well coated and dressing is hot. Remove from heat and transfer to a serving bowl. Serve immediately.

1 serving: *220 Calories; 16 g Total Fat (8 g Mono, 2 g Poly, 5 g Sat); 20 mg Cholesterol; 14 g Carbohydrate (4 g Fibre; 5 g Sugar); 7 g Protein; 350 mg Sodium*

Honey and Herb Brined Turkey

Serves 15

More and more people are turning to brining to ensure a moist and flavourful turkey, and it really is the best way. If you haven't tried it yet, now's the time. You'll get the best results from brining for 18 hours, but you'll notice benefits from as little as a two-hour dip in the brine. We don't recommend stuffing your brined turkey, because you're likely to end up with stuffing that is too salty. Cook it separately instead.

8 quarts (8 L) warm water

2 cups (500 mL) coarse salt

1 cup (250 mL) honey

1/3 cup (75 mL) lightly packed sprigs of fresh rosemary

1/3 cup (75 mL) lightly packed fresh thyme sprigs

1/3 cup (75 mL) fresh sage leaves

8 cloves garlic

2 Tbsp (30 mL) cracked black pepper

1 x 18 to 20 lb (8 to 9 kg) turkey

1/2 cup (125 mL) butter

salt and freshly ground pepper to taste

For the brine, combine water and salt in a large stockpot. Stir until salt has dissolved. Add honey and stir until combined. Stir in rosemary, thyme, sage, garlic and cracked black pepper. Add turkey. Place a large, heavy plate on top of turkey to submerge it completely in brine. Refrigerate for 12 to 18 hours.

Preheat oven to 450°F (230°C). Drain turkey well and discard brine. Pat turkey dry inside and out. Tuck wings under turkey and tie legs together loosely. Transfer to rack in a roasting pan. Rub turkey with butter and sprinkle generously with salt and pepper. Place roasting pan in oven. Reduce oven temperature to 325°F (160°C). Roast until thermometer inserted into thickest part of thigh registers 175°F (80°C), about 2 1/2 hours. Transfer to a serving platter and tent with foil. Let turkey rest at least 30 minutes before carving (internal temperature will rise while standing, bringing your bird up to or past the 180°F, 82°C, mark for fully cooked poultry).

1 serving: 620 Calories; 33 g Total Fat (11 g Mono, 7 g Poly, 12 g Sat); 280 mg Cholesterol; 3 g Carbohydrate (0 g Fibre, 2 g Sugar); 74 g Protein; 1730 mg Sodium

Tip

If you don't have a stockpot big enough to fit your turkey, line a cooler with a large, clean, heavy-duty plastic garbage bag. Place turkey and brine inside bag. Cover turkey with plate to submerge, then tie up the bag and close the cooler lid. Place cooler in refrigerator.

If the stockpot doesn't fit in your refrigerator, use the cooler option above, and keep it in a cool place (about 39°F, 4°C), such as a garage. If you think the cool place might not be cold enough, monitor the temperature every few hours and add freezer packs to your cooler as necessary.

Pear Gravy

Makes 3 3/4 cups (925 mL)

While turkey is resting, make gravy. Spoon off fat from pan drippings, reserving 1/4 cup (60 mL) fat. Measure out 2/3 cup (150 mL) pan juices. In a large saucepan over medium heat, melt butter and reserved 1/4 cup (60 mL) fat. Stir in flour. Cook, stirring constantly, until light brown, about 2 minutes. Whisk in broth, pear juice and reserved 2/3 cup (150 mL) pan juices. Simmer, stirring, until thickened, about 10 minutes. Stir in rum. Season with salt and pepper.

1/4 cup (60 mL): 90 Calories; 7 g Total Fat (3 g Mono, 1 g Poly, 2 g Sat); 10 mg Cholesterol; 5 g Carbohydrate (0 g Fibre, 2 g Sugar); 1 g Protein; 160 mg Sodium

1/4 cup (60 mL) butter

1/2 cup (125 mL) all-purpose flour

2 cups (500 mL) low-sodium chicken broth

1 cup (250 mL) pear juice

2 Tbsp (30 mL) dark rum

salt and freshly ground pepper to taste

Oka and Cranberry-stuffed Turkey Breast

Serves 5

Oka is Canada's most famous native cheese, first produced in 1893 by Trappist monks who had been exiled from France and found a new home in Oka, Quebec. It is a surface-ripened semi-soft cheese with a creamy texture and pungent aroma that stands out on a cheese platter. It has a fruity, nutty flavour and melts beautifully, as you'll see in this recipe. If you are cooking for two, this recipe can easily be halved.

1/2 cup (125 mL) grated Oka cheese

1/4 cup (60 mL) dried cranberries, chopped

1/4 cup (60 mL) chopped roasted walnuts

2 Tbsp (30 mL) chopped fresh sage

1/4 tsp (1 mL) *each* salt and freshly ground pepper

2 turkey breast scallopine (see Tip)

1 Tbsp (15 mL) grape seed oil

Preheat oven to 350°F (175°C). Combine cheese, cranberries, walnuts, sage, salt and pepper in small bowl. Lay turkey breast scallopines on work surface. Cover each scallopine with half the stuffing, leaving 1 inch (2.5 cm) border around the edges. Bring the long edges together to form a tight roll. Tie around the roll with butcher's twine every 2 inches (5 cm), and wrap once around the length to hold the shape while cooking.

Heat oil in a large ovenproof saucepan over medium-high. Sear turkey breast rolls until golden brown on all sides. Transfer pan to oven and roast until cooked through, about 15 minutes. Remove from oven. Cut twine and slice crosswise into 1 inch (2.5 cm) slices. Serve with rice and other seasonal side dishes.

1 serving: 480 Calories; 26 g Total Fat (8 g Mono, 9 g Poly, 7 g Sat); 155 mg Cholesterol; 6 g Carbohydrates; trace Fibre; 4 g Sugar; 54 g Protein; 270 mg Sodium

Tip

These scallopine are simply turkey breasts that have been cut to half thickness. If you cannot find turkey scallopine at your grocer, buy a whole turkey breast and make the cut at home.

Cider-glazed Roast Duck

Serves 4

Whole ducks are usually available in grocery stores (if you can't find one at yours, try an Asian grocer), and roast duck is an exciting alternative to other birds. The higher fat content ensures a moist and tender meat, but much of the excess fat is cooked off during the roasting process. Keep leftover duck fat sealed and refrigerated for up to 6 months to use in place of oil or butter for roasted or sautéed root vegetables and squash.

1 x 5 to 6 lb (2.3 to 2.7 kg) Long Island or Pekin duck, excess fat discarded

1 Tbsp (15 mL) coarse salt

1 Gala apple, cored and quartered

1/4 cup (60 mL) plus 1 Tbsp (15 mL) sugar, *divided*

1 cup (250 mL) apple cider

1/2 cup (125 mL) cider vinegar

3 Tbsp (45 mL) minced shallots

2 tsp (10 mL) cornstarch

1 1/2 Tbsp (22 mL) Calvados

salt and freshly ground pepper to taste

Preheat oven to 350°F (175°C). Separate duck skin and fat from breast meat: from large cavity end, carefully work your fingers between skin and meat, without tearing skin. Use a fork to prick duck skin and fat all over. Rub inside and out with coarse salt. Stuff apple quarters into cavity. Place, breast side up, in a medium roasting pan. Sprinkle 1/4 cup (60 mL) sugar around duck. Pour boiling water over duck until water level reaches about halfway up duck (but at least 1 inch, 2.5 cm, from top of roasting pan). Cover tightly with foil. Braise 1 hour. Remove pan from oven.

Remove foil and set aside. Carefully turn duck over. Cover again with foil and return to oven until meat is very tender but not falling off the bone, about 1 more hour. Remove from oven.

Drain any juices from inside duck into pan, and transfer duck to platter. Transfer cooking liquid to a large bowl. Cool duck and liquid separately, uncovered, to room temperature, then transfer both to refrigerator, uncovered, to chill for at least 4 hours or overnight.

Remove fat from chilled cooking liquid and set aside for another use. Combine cider, vinegar and 1 Tbsp (15 mL) sugar in a small saucepan. Boil until darkened and reduced to about 3 Tbsp (45 mL), about 10 minutes. Reserve about 2 tsp (10 mL) glaze in a cup to brush on duck. Stir 1 cup (250 mL) reserved cooking liquid into remaining glaze and set aside. Reserve 1 cup (250 mL) of remaining cooking liquid and discard the rest.

Preheat oven to 500°F (260°C). Transfer duck to a rack in a roasting pan. Roast until skin is crisp, about 25 to 35 minutes. Remove from oven. Transfer to serving platter. Brush duck with reserved glaze. Let stand at least 10 minutes before serving.

Pour off and discard all but 2 tsp (10 mL) fat from roasting pan. Set pan on stovetop over medium-low heat. Add shallots and cook, stirring, until light gold, about 3 to 5 minutes. Deglaze with reserved cooking liquid, stirring and scraping up brown bits for 2 minutes. Remove from heat and pour through a fine-mesh sieve into saucepan with glaze mixture. Bring to a boil over medium-high heat. Stir cornstarch into Calvados and add to sauce. Reduce heat and simmer, stirring occasionally, until thickened, about 3 to 5 minutes. Season with salt and pepper. Serve duck with sauce alongside.

1 serving: 950 Calories; 60 g Total Fat (27 g Mono, 8 g Poly, 20 g Sat); 320 mg Cholesterol; 24 g Carbohydrate (1 g Fibre, 17 g Sugar); 70 g Protein; 1900 mg Sodium

Dinde au Vin avec Crème

Serves 6

Our twist on the traditional Coq au Vin uses turkey instead of chicken. It may come as a surprise that using white wine instead of red is not a twist on the classic, which actually calls for a local wine, red or white. A dry white wine, whether from B.C. or Ontario, makes for a smooth and mellow sauce that beautifully complements the rich flavour of the turkey. Avoid wine with a strong oak flavour because it will conflict with the other flavours in the dish. And make sure you buy more than just the bottle called for in the recipe—the ideal accompaniment for this dish is, of course, a glass of white wine.

1/4 lb (113 g) bacon

2 large onions, diced into 1/2 inch (12 mm) pieces

3 lbs (1.4 kg) turkey pieces, preferably bone in

1/4 cup (60 mL) flour

3 Tbsp (45 mL) butter, optional

1 x 750 mL bottle of dry white wine

3 oz (80 g) dried mushrooms, rehydrated in boiling water

4 cloves garlic, minced

bouquet garni (see p. 69) or use 4 bay leaves

salt and freshly ground pepper to taste

2 cups (500 mL) Homemade Crème Fraîche (see opposite)

chopped flat-leaf parsley, for garnish

Cook bacon in a medium saucepan over medium heat until crisp. Remove from pan and set aside. Add onions to pan. Cook, stirring, until golden. Remove and set aside with bacon. Coat turkey pieces with flour on all sides. Add to saucepan and cook until golden brown on all sides (if there is not enough bacon fat left in the pan, melt butter in saucepan before adding turkey pieces). Add wine, mushrooms, garlic, bouquet garni and bacon and onions. Season with salt and pepper. Simmer, uncovered, for 30 minutes. Stir in crème fraîche. Cover and simmer for another 30 minutes or until turkey pieces are tender. Garnish with parsley. Serve with potatoes or rice.

1 serving: 780 Calories; 46 g Total Fat (15 g Mono, 4.5 g Poly, 22 g Sat); 235 mg Cholesterol; 26 g Carbohydrates (2 g Fibre, 8 g Sugar); 96 g Protein; 420 mg Sodium

Homemade Crème Fraîche

Makes 2 cups (500 mL)

Combine whipping cream and yogurt in a sterile glass jar. Mix well. Cover tightly. Let sit overnight or 12 hours in a warm place to thicken. Refrigerate for up to 2 weeks.

1/4 cup (60 mL): 140 Calories; 14 g Total Fat (4 g Mono, 0 g Poly, 9 g Sat); 55 mg Cholesterol; 2 g Carbohydrate (0 g Fibre, trace Sugar); 2 g Protein; 25 mg Sodium

1 1/2 cups (375 mL) whipping cream

1/2 cup (125 mL) plain yogurt (with active cultures)

Maple Black Pepper Quail

Serves 4

They say good things come in small packages, and that's certainly true of these quail. Tender and moist, with a warming maple glaze, they cook quickly and make for an elegant presentation. If you're not lucky enough to find locally raised quail at your farmers' market, try an Asian grocer. Crisp roasted potatoes make the perfect accompaniment for this dish.

2 Tbsp (30 mL) butter, *divided*

2 Tbsp (30 mL) grape seed oil, *divided*

8 quail

1 tsp (5 mL) salt

1/4 tsp (1 mL) freshly ground pepper

1 Tbsp (15 mL) whole black peppercorns

3/4 cup (175 mL) chicken broth, *divided*

1/4 cup (60 mL) maple syrup

10 x 3 inch (7.5 cm) sprigs of fresh rosemary, *divided*

1/4 cup (60 mL) balsamic vinegar

2 Tbsp (30 mL) cold butter

Preheat oven to 350°F (175°C). Heat 1 Tbsp (15 mL) each butter and grape seed oil in heavy sauté pan on medium until foam subsides. Season quail with salt and pepper. Brown 4 quail on all sides, about 10 minutes in total. Transfer to a baking pan. Wipe sauté pan clean and repeat with remaining 4 quail. Roast until cooked through, about 5 to 10 minutes depending on size.

Toast peppercorns in a dry, heavy sauté pan over medium heat until fragrant, about 3 minutes. Transfer to work surface and crush with a rolling pin. Return crushed peppercorns to pan. Add 1/2 cup (125 mL) chicken broth, maple syrup and 2 sprigs of rosemary. Simmer 20 minutes.

Remove quail from pan and transfer to a serving platter. Deglaze sauté pan with balsamic vinegar. Cook until reduced by half. Stir in maple syrup mixture and remaining broth. Simmer until reduced and thickened to a syrupy consistency. Reduce heat to low. Swirl in butter. Taste and add salt if necessary. Strain and pour over quail. Garnish each quail with a sprig of rosemary.

1 serving: 600 Calories; 46 g Total Fat (14 g Mono, 12 g Poly, 16 g Sat); 195 mg Cholesterol; 17 g Carbohydrate (4 g Fibre, 12 g Sugar); 44 g Protein; 910 mg Sodium

Seared Scallops with Mushrooms and Leeks

Serves 4

Earthy mushrooms and mild leeks bring out the full flavours of scallops at their peak in this easy elegant dish, which is ready in no time. For a dish this simple, be sure to use the freshest of ingredients.

1 leek (white and pale green parts only), washed well

2 cups (500 mL) oyster mushrooms

1 Tbsp (15 mL) olive oil

12 to 20 sea scallops, depending on size, patted very dry

pinch *each* of salt and freshly ground black pepper

2 cups (500 mL) Homemade Fish Stock (see opposite) or Homemade Vegetable Stock (see p. 77)

Julienne leek into 1 1/2 x 1/2 inch (3.8 x 12 mm) strips. Tear oyster mushrooms into strips.

Heat olive oil in a large sauté pan over high. Sprinkle scallops with salt and pepper. Quickly sear scallops to golden brown on both flat sides. Reduce heat to medium. Add leeks and mushrooms. Sauté until just softened, about 1 or 2 minutes. Add stock and simmer, uncovered, until scallops are just cooked through, about 4 to 8 minutes. Remove from heat. Divide leeks and mushrooms evenly among 4 soup plates. Nestle scallops on top and pour broth over.

1 serving: 280 Calories; 5 g Total Fat (2.5 g Mono, 1 g Poly, 0.5 g Sat); 80 mg Cholesterol; 12 g Carbohydrate (2 g Fibre, 1 g Sugar); 41 g Protein; 610 mg Sodium

Homemade Fish Stock

Makes 8 cups (2 L)

Rinse any blood off fish bones. In a large saucepan combine bones, wine and just enough water to cover, and bring to a boil over medium-high heat. Skim foam that rises to surface. Add remaining ingredients and more water to cover, if necessary. Reduce heat and cook just below simmer for about 20 minutes. Strain through colander and discard solids. Strain again through a cheesecloth-lined fine-mesh sieve. Discard solids. Season very lightly with salt. If not using immediately, cool, uncovered, to room temperature, then chill, covered; keep in refrigerator for up to 3 days or freeze for up to 3 months.

1 cup (250 mL): 30 Calories; 0 g Total Fat (0 g Mono, 0 g Poly, 0 g Sat); 1 mg Cholesterol; 1 g Carbohydrate (0 g Fibre; 0 g Sugar); 3 g Protein; 310 mg Sodium

4 lbs (1.8 kg) fish bones, cut into 2 inch (5 cm) sections

1/2 cup (125 mL) dry white wine

8 cups (2 L) water, *divided*

2 medium yellow onions, sliced thin

4 stalks celery, sliced thin

2 medium carrots, sliced thin

2 bay leaves

1/4 cup (60 mL) coarsely chopped flat-leaf parsley

8 sprigs of fresh thyme

2 Tbsp (30 mL) whole black peppercorns

salt to taste

Salmon in Puff Pastry with Cranberry Dill Sauce

Serves 4

A dill-scented cranberry sauce provides a tart contrast to salmon wrapped in rich puff pastry. Cooking the salmon in the pastry seals in all the juices and ensures a moist and tender piece of fish. Make the Cranberry Dill Sauce the day before you plan to make the salmon recipe.

1 package of frozen puff pastry (2 sheets), thawed

4 x 3/4 inch (2 cm) thick skinless salmon fillets, about 6 oz (170 g) each

salt and freshly ground pepper to taste

1/4 cup (60 mL) lemon juice, *divided*

1/4 cup (60 mL) chopped fresh dill, *divided*

1 egg, beaten (for glaze)

Preheat oven to 425°F (220°C). Roll out each pastry sheet on lightly floured surface to 12 inches (30 cm) square. Cut each in half, forming four 12 x 6 inch (30 x 15 cm) rectangles. Place 1 salmon fillet in centre of each rectangle, about 3 inches (7.5 cm) in from and parallel to short edge. Sprinkle each fillet with salt, pepper, 1 Tbsp (15 mL) lemon juice and 1 Tbsp (15 mL) dill. Brush edges of rectangles with egg glaze. Fold long sides of pastry over fillets. Fold short edge of pastry over fillets and roll up pastry, enclosing fillets. Seal edges of pastry. Place pastries, seam side down, on baking sheet. Brush with glaze.

Bake pastries until dough is golden brown, about 20 minutes. Remove from oven; let stand 10 minutes. Cut pastries into thirds and transfer to plates. Drizzle Cranberry Dill Sauce overtop or serve on the side.

1 serving: 940 Calories; 55 g Total Fat (29 g Mono, 10 g Poly, 13 g Sat); 145 mg Cholesterol; 66 g Carbohydrate (3 g Fibre, 13 g Sugar); 44 g Protein; 600 mg Sodium

Cranberry Dill Sauce

Makes 2 cups (500 mL)

Combine cranberries, onion, pepper, syrup, ginger and salt in medium saucepan on medium-low heat. Cook, stirring, until cranberries start to pop, about 10 to 15 minutes. Stir in dill. Purée with hand blender, then return to heat and cook until slightly thickened, about 5 minutes more. Set aside.

1/2 cup (125 mL): 50 Calories; 0 g Total Fat (0 g Mono, 0 g Poly, 0 g Sat); 0 mg Cholesterol; 14 g Carbohydrate (2 g Fibre, 12 g Sugar); 0 g Protein; 75 mg Sodium

1 cup (250 mL) fresh or frozen cranberries

1/4 cup (60 mL) diced red onion

1/2 cup (125 mL) diced green pepper

1/4 cup (60 mL) maple syrup

1 tsp (5 mL) grated ginger

pinch of salt

2 Tbsp (30 mL) chopped fresh dill

Crown Roast of Pork with Autumn Fruit

Serves 9

Humans have been pairing apples with pork for centuries, with good reason. The tart-sweetness of the fruit balances the richness of the meat. A crown roast of pork makes a beautifully elegant presentation and is no more difficult to make than any other roast. The one extra step? Ordering the crown roast from your butcher.

3 Tbsp (45 mL) ground allspice

3 Tbsp (45 mL) fennel seeds, lightly crushed

2 Tbsp (30 mL) red pepper flakes

2 Tbsp (30 mL) plus 1/4 tsp (1 mL) salt, *divided*

1 x 12 rib crown roast of pork

4 medium apples, cored and cut into 1/2 inch (12 mm) slices

4 medium firm pears, cored and cut into 1/2 inch (12 mm) slices

2 Tbsp (30 mL) lemon juice

1 Tbsp (15 mL) chopped fresh sage

1 Tbsp (15 mL) chopped fresh thyme

1/4 tsp (1 mL) freshly ground pepper

Preheat oven to 325°F (160°C). Combine allspice, fennel seeds, pepper flakes and 2 Tbsp (30 mL) salt in a small bowl. Place roast, bones up, in a shallow roasting pan. Pat dry. Rub all over with spice mixture. Fill cavity with a large ball of crumpled foil and cover bone tips with small pieces of foil. Roast, uncovered, for 1 1/2 hours.

In a large bowl, toss fruit with lemon juice, sage, thyme, 1/4 tsp (1 mL) salt and pepper. Remove roast from oven. Drain off excess fat. Remove foil ball from cavity and fill cavity with fruit. Arrange remaining fruit in pan around roast. Return to oven and roast until meat thermometer inserted into the thickest part of the meat (not touching bones) registers 160°F (71°C), about 1 to 1 1/2 hours more.

Remove from oven. Let stand, tented with foil, for 25 minutes before carving. Serve with the cooked fruit alongside.

1 serving: 940 Calories; 55 g Total Fat (0 g Mono, 0 g Poly, 23 g Sat); 270 mg Cholesterol; 21 g Carbohydrate (5 g Fibre, 13 g Sugar); 95 g Protein; 3110 mg Sodium

The image of a whole roast pig with an apple in its mouth is familiar to just about everyone. It was believed that the acidity of the apples helped to digest fatty meats like pork. The validity of that idea is questionable, but they certainly taste good together.

Pork Tenderloin Medallions with Blackberry Balsamic Sauce

Serves 5

Pork tenderloin is an extremely lean and healthy meat—almost as low in fat as chicken breast. It's just as quick to cook, making for easy, speedy weeknight meals. This recipe goes from fridge to table in under 20 minutes, including the tangy blackberry sauce. But because it's so low in fat, be careful not to overcook your tenderloin or it will come out tough.

2 lbs (900 g) pork tenderloin

1/2 tsp (2 mL) *each* salt and freshly ground black pepper

1 Tbsp (15 mL) grape seed oil

Slice tenderloins crosswise into 1 inch (2.5 cm) thick medallions. Sprinkle both sides with salt and pepper. Heat oil in a large sauté pan over medium-high. Sear medallions to brown, cooking about 2 minutes on each side. Lower heat to medium. Cook, turning occasionally, until cooked through (155°F, 65°C, on a meat thermometer), about 10 minutes more. Fan medallions on 5 plates or a serving platter and drizzle with sauce.

1 serving with 1/3 cup (75 mL) sauce: 350 Calories; 13 g Total Fat (5 g Mono, 3 g Poly, 3.5 g Sat); 120 mg Cholesterol; 20 g Carbohydrate (trace Fibre, 19 g Sugar) 37 g Protein; 380 mg Sodium

Blackberry Balsamic Sauce
Makes 3 cups (750 mL)

Combine all ingredients in a small saucepan. Bring to a low simmer and cook until mixture is reduced by about half and coats the back of a spoon. Use a wooden spoon to press sauce through a fine-mesh sieve, and set aside.

1/3 cup (75 mL): 160 Calories; 0 g Total Fat (0 g Mono, 0 g Poly, 0 g Sat); 0 mg Cholesterol; 39 g Carbohydrate (2 g Fibre, 37 g Sugar); 0 g Protein; 105 mg Sodium

1 cup (250 mL) balsamic vinegar

1 cup (250 mL) blackberries, and a few more for garnish

3/4 cup (175 mL) sugar

1/4 tsp (1 mL) sea salt

Roast Bison with Juniper Berry Gravy

Serves 8

Bison is a healthier alternative to beef, and it has a wonderful flavour when cooked properly. Don't be intimidated—all it needs is a lower cooking temperature and a little more careful clock-watching. Bison, like other game meat, is very lean and toughens quickly when overcooked. It is best served rare to medium-rare and should never be cooked past medium.

3 Tbsp (45 mL) juniper berries

2 Tbsp (30 mL) whole black peppercorns

4 whole cloves

1 tsp (5 mL) fennel seeds

1 tsp (5 mL) coriander seeds

1 Tbsp (15 mL) grape seed oil

1 x 4 lb (1.8 kg) bison sirloin roast

1 Tbsp (15 mL) salt

Preheat oven to 275°F (140°C). Finely grind juniper berries, peppercorns, cloves, fennel seeds and coriander seeds in a spice grinder. Lightly oil roast, sprinkle with salt, and rub all over with spice mixture.

Heat a large sauté pan over medium-high. Sear roast to brown on all sides. Transfer to a shallow roasting pan. Roast until internal temperature reaches 120°F (49°C) for rare, about 1 hour. Transfer to a serving platter to rest, tented with foil, for at least 20 minutes before slicing.

1 serving with 1/4 cup (60 mL) gravy: 300 Calories; 7 g Total Fat (2.5 g Mono, 2 g Poly, 2 g Sat); 160 mg Cholesterol; 3 g Carbohydrate (0 g Fibre, 0 g Sugar); 49 g Protein; 1070 mg Sodium

Juniper Berry Gravy

Makes 2 cups (500 mL)

Add broth, wine, water and juniper berries to roasting pan set over medium-high heat. Simmer, stirring and scraping up brown bits, for 5 minutes. Strain through a fine-mesh sieve into a small saucepan over medium heat. Stir cornstarch into water until dissolved, then add to mixture in small saucepan along with balsamic vinegar. Season to taste with salt and pepper. Simmer, whisking constantly, for 5 minutes. Serve alongside bison.

1/4 cup (60 mL): 20 Calories; 0 g Total Fat (0 g Mono, 0 g Poly, 0 g Sat); 0 mg Cholesterol; 2 g Carbohydrate (0 g Fibre, 0 g Sugar); 0 g Protein; 80 mg Sodium

1/2 cup (125 mL) beef broth

1/2 cup (125 mL) red wine

1/2 cup (125 mL) water

1 Tbsp (15 mL) juniper berries, lightly crushed

2 tsp (10 mL) cornstarch

2 Tbsp (30 mL) water

1 Tbsp (15 mL) balsamic vinegar

salt and freshly ground pepper to taste

Grilled Venison Steaks with Chanterelles and Chestnuts

Serves 4

Venison, like bison, is a very lean meat that must be cooked at a lower temperature than beef to avoid overcooking. These steaks need to be marinated for six hours or overnight, so keep that in mind when planning this recipe. Cook these steaks rare to medium-rare, never past medium. Sautéed chanterelles and chestnuts add an earthy flavour to the steaks.

3 Tbsp (45 mL) olive oil

1 Tbsp (15 mL) soy sauce

1 Tbsp (15 mL) lemon juice

1 Tbsp (15 mL) Worcestershire sauce

2 cloves garlic, minced

1 Tbsp (15 mL) minced shallots

freshly ground black pepper, to taste

4 x 8 oz (225 g) venison steaks

2 Tbsp (30 mL) butter

1 cup (250 mL) roasted chopped chestnuts (see Tip)

2 cups (500 mL) chanterelles, torn into strips

salt to taste

For the marinade combine oil, soy sauce, lemon juice, Worcestershire sauce, garlic, shallots and pepper in a shallow pan and mix well. Add venison steaks and turn to coat. Cover and refrigerate, turning occasionally, for at least 6 hours or overnight.

Preheat grill to medium. Remove steaks from marinade and grill about 3 to 5 minutes per side, depending on thickness. Transfer to platter, cover with foil and let rest 5 minutes before serving.

Meanwhile, heat butter in large sauté pan over medium. Add chestnuts and chanterelles and cook, stirring, until they begin to colour, about 5 minutes. Season with salt and pepper. Remove from heat and serve on top of venison steaks.

1 serving: *520 Calories; 22 g Total Fat (11 g Mono, 2.5 g Poly, 7 g Sat); 210 mg Cholesterol; 23 g Carbohydrate (2 g Fibre, 5 g Sugar); 55 g Protein; 510 mg Sodium*

Tip

To roast chestnuts, preheat oven to 350°F (175°C). Use a chestnut knife or sharp paring knife to cut a large X on flat side of each chestnut. Be careful to cut only through the shell, not the meat. Place chestnuts in a medium bowl and add warm water to cover by 2 inches (5 cm). Soak for 15 minutes, then drain well. Roast in a single layer in a shallow baking pan on middle rack of oven until shells curl away at the X mark, about 15 minutes. Wearing gloves, peel shells from chestnuts while still hot. Blanch chestnuts in boiling water 2 minutes and drain. Rub with a kitchen towel to remove furry skins.

Elk Bourguignon

Serves 8

This northern twist on the classic French dish of beef cooked in red wine replaces the beef with elk for even more flavour. This recipes taste even better the next day.

3 lbs (1.4 kg) boneless elk stewing meat, cut into 2 inch (5 cm) chunks

salt and freshly ground black pepper to taste

1/3 cup (75 mL) all-purpose flour

2 Tbsp (30 mL) grape seed oil, *divided*

4 1/2 Tbsp (67 mL) butter, *divided*

1/2 cup (125 mL) brandy

3 slices thick-sliced bacon, cut 1 inch (2.5 cm) wide

2 onions, finely chopped

3 large cloves garlic, minced

2 carrots, very thinly sliced

1 Tbsp (15 mL) tomato paste

1 x 750 mL bottle of dry red wine

bouquet garni (see Tip)

1 lb (454 g) pearl onions, blanched and peeled (see p. 122)

1 1/2 cups (375 mL) water

1 lb (454 g) mushrooms, trimmed, quartered if large

Pat elk pieces dry and sprinkle with salt and pepper. Divide flour into 2 large resealable plastic bags. Divide elk between the bags, seal bags and shake to coat.

Heat 1 1/2 Tbsp (22 mL) oil and 1 1/2 Tbsp (22 mL) butter in large saucepan over medium, until hot but not smoking. Working in batches, without crowding, brown elk meat well on all sides. Add remaining oil as needed. Once browned, transfer to a large bowl. Pour off excess oil from pan. Deglaze with brandy, stirring and scraping up any brown bits, for 1 minute. Pour over meat in bowl.

Heat 1 Tbsp (15 mL) butter in cleaned saucepan over medium-high until foam subsides. Add bacon and cook, stirring, for 2 minutes. Add chopped onions, garlic and carrots and cook, stirring occasionally, until light golden, about 5 minutes. Add tomato paste. Cook, stirring, for 1 minute. Add wine, meat and its juices and bouquet garni. Simmer gently, partially covered, until meat is tender, about 3 1/2 to 4 hours.

Heat 1 Tbsp (15 mL) butter in medium saucepan over medium-high until foam subsides. Add pearl onions and cook, stirring occasionally, until browned in patches. Season with salt and pepper. Add water. Simmer, partially covered, until onions are tender, about 15 minutes. Increase heat and boil, uncovered, stirring occasionally, until liquid is reduced to a glaze, 5 to 10 minutes. Remove from heat.

Heat remaining 1 Tbsp (15 mL) butter in a medium sauté pan over medium-high until foam subsides. Add mushrooms. Cook, stirring, until golden brown and any liquid has evaporated, 6 to 8 minutes. Remove from heat.

Once meat is tender, stir onions and mushrooms into stew. Simmer for 10 minutes. Remove and discard bouquet garni. Skim any fat from surface and season stew to taste with salt and pepper.

1 serving: *560 Calories: 21 g Total Fat (7 g Mono, 4.5 g Poly, 8 g Sat); 125 mg Cholesterol; 22 g Carbohydrate (2 g Fibre, 6 g Sugar); 45 g Protein; 490 mg Sodium*

Tip

To make a bouquet garni, stick 2 whole cloves into a 4 inch (10 cm) piece of celery. Tie celery with 4 stems fresh parsley (without leaves), 4 sprigs fresh thyme and 2 bay leaves.

Beef Sirloin Roast with Gorgonzola Gravy

Serves 7

Roast beef has long been a Canadian Sunday-dinner favourite. Make yours extraordinary by rubbing the meat with a homemade spice rub before roasting and serving with a Gorgonzola gravy. Serve with roast potatoes, Yorkshire puddings or other favourite accompaniments for a true feast.

1 1/4 tsp (6 mL) paprika

1 Tbsp (15 mL) kosher salt

1 tsp (5 mL) cracked black pepper

1/2 tsp (2 mL) cayenne pepper

1/2 tsp (2 mL) dried oregano

1/2 tsp (2 mL) dried thyme

2 Tbsp (30 mL) olive oil

1 x 3 to 5 lb (1.4 to 2.3 kg) sirloin roast

1 cup (250 mL) beef broth

1 Tbsp (15 mL) cornstarch

2 Tbsp (30 mL) Madeira

1/4 cup (60 mL) crumbled Gorgonzola cheese

salt and freshly ground pepper to taste

Preheat oven to 300°F (150°C). In a small bowl, combine paprika, kosher salt, cracked pepper, cayenne, oregano and thyme. Stir in olive oil. Let sit 15 minutes. Rub roast with spice mixture. Heat a large sauté pan over medium-high. Sear roast on all sides to brown, about 10 minutes. Transfer to rack in a roasting pan. Roast for about 10 minutes per pound, until meat reaches an internal temperature of 120°F (49°C) for rare, 135°F (57°C) for medium-rare or 150°F (65°C) for medium. Transfer to serving platter and rest, tented with foil, for 15 minutes before slicing and serving.

To make gravy, spoon off and discard fat from drippings in roasting pan. Set pan on stovetop over medium-high heat. Deglaze with beef broth. Bring to a boil, stirring and scraping up brown bits. Whisk cornstarch into Madeira. Add to pan. Cook, stirring, until thickened, about 3 minutes. Stir in Gorgonzola until melted. Season with salt and pepper. Serve alongside roast. Garnish with grapes and additional Gorgonzola, if desired.

1 serving: 490 Calories; 35 g Total Fat (17 g Mono, 1.5 g Poly, 14 g Sat); 140 mg Cholesterol; 2 g Carbohydrate (0 g Fibre, 0 g Sugar); 41 g Protein; 1310 mg Sodium

Gorgonzola is a soft, crumbly blue cheese that originates from the Gorgonzola region of northern Italy. It comes in two varieties: Gorgonzola dolce, or sweet Gorgonzola, which has a milder flavour, and Gorgonzola piccante, or mountain Gorgonzola, which has a sharper taste.

Quinoa-stuffed Vine Leaves

Serves 4

If you've ever been to a Greek holiday dinner, or dined in a Greek restaurant, you'll know that dolmades are usually stuffed with a ground beef and rice mixture. Our vegetarian version substitutes quinoa for the rice to pack a protein punch. Serve with lemon wedges and Balkan-style yogurt.

1 1/4 cups (300 mL) uncooked quinoa

1/4 cup (60 mL) chopped sun-dried tomatoes

1/4 cup (60 mL) chopped roasted yellow peppers (see p. 33)

1/4 cup (60 mL) chopped fresh flat-leaf parsley

2 tsp (10 mL) chopped fresh oregano

2 tsp (10 mL) lemon zest

1/2 tsp (2 mL) *each* salt and freshly ground pepper

1 x 16 oz (545 g) jar brined grape vine leaves, carefully separated and rinsed well

2 cups (500 mL) boiling water

Preheat oven to 350°F (175°C). Combine quinoa, sun-dried tomatoes, roasted peppers, parsley, oregano, lemon zest, salt and pepper in a medium bowl.

Carefully separate vine leaves. Place each leaf, shiny side down and stem toward you, on work surface. Put 1 Tbsp (15 mL) stuffing near bottom of leaf. Fold bottom and sides inward to cover filling, then roll tightly toward tip of leaf. Pack tightly, seam side down, into baking dish. Pour boiling water into baking dish. Cover vine leaves with a plate to keep them from unrolling during cooking. Bake until quinoa is tender, about 30 minutes. Drain and serve.

1 serving: 310 Calories; 5 g Total Fat (1 g Mono, 3 g Poly, 0.5 g Sat); 0 mg Cholesterol; 55 g Carbohydrate (16 g Fibre, 8 g Sugar); 13 g Protein; 420 mg Sodium

Grape vine leaves come already brined in jars. They should be rinsed before use; just swish them gently around in a sink half filled with cold water and then drain them well.

Stuffed Acorn Squash

Serves 2

This vegetarian entrée is so chock-full of seasonal bounty that it could replace the cornucopia on the autumn table. Vegetarians sitting down to a holiday meal will feel as though this time they got the beautiful showpiece.

1 x 1 1/2 lb (680 g) acorn squash

salt and freshly ground pepper to taste

1/2 cup (125 mL) dried cranberries

1/4 cup (60 mL) hot water

3 Tbsp (45 mL) butter

1/4 cup (60 mL) chopped onion

4 oz (113 g) shiitake mushrooms

1 tsp (5 mL) chopped fresh sage

1 tsp (5 mL) chopped fresh thyme

1/2 cup (125 mL) corn kernels

1/2 cup (125 mL) cooked assorted beans, such as cranberry beans and navy beans

1/2 cup (125 mL) cooked wild rice

Remove top of squash by cutting a circle about 2 inches (5 cm) in diameter around the stem with a sharp knife. Reserve lid. Scrape out and discard seeds and pulp. Sprinkle flesh with salt and pepper. Transfer to a roasting pan.

Preheat oven to 425°F (220°C). Soften cranberries in hot water. Melt butter in a large saucepan over medium heat. Add onion, mushrooms, sage and thyme. Sauté until beginning to soften, about 5 minutes. Stir in corn and cook for another 2 minutes. Remove from heat. Add beans, wild rice and cranberries with their soaking liquid. Season with salt and pepper.

Mound stuffing into squash cavity. Put lid on top of squash. Roast on middle rack of oven until squash is tender and stuffing is heated through, about 45 minutes to 1 hour. Transfer to platter. To serve, scoop out a portion of stuffing along with some of the squash flesh.

1 serving: 550 Calories; 19 g Total Fat (4.5 g Mono, 1 g Poly, 11 g Sat); 45 mg Cholesterol; 91 g Carbohydrate (15 g Fibre, 34 g Sugar); 12 g Protein; 790 mg Sodium

Tip

If you can't find fresh shiitake mushrooms, look for
a small packet of dried shiitakes in the shelves of the
produce section of your supermarket. Soak them in hot
water for 20 minutes or so, and then prepare them as
directed in this recipe. You may wish to discard the stems
if they are tough.

Cannellini and Kale Ragout

Serves 4

Ragout is traditionally a thick, rich stew of meat, poultry or fish, with or without vegetables, meant to stimulate the appetite. We've turned tradition on its ear and kept the vegetables, but eliminated the meat. You won't even miss it, and this recipe might stimulate your appetite enough to make you come back for seconds.

6 Tbsp (90 mL) extra virgin olive oil, *divided*

4 x 1 1/2 inch (3.8 cm) thick slices Italian bread, crusts removed, each slice quartered

1 tsp (5 mL) plus 1 Tbsp (15 mL) chopped fresh thyme, *divided*

salt and freshly ground pepper to taste

4 cloves garlic, minced

1/2 tsp (2 mL) dried crushed red pepper

1 large bunch of kale, thinly sliced

1 1/2 cups (375 mL) Homemade Vegetable Stock (see opposite)

1 x 14 oz (398 mL) can of crushed tomatoes

1 1/2 cups (375 mL) cooked cannellini beans

Heat 2 Tbsp (30 mL) oil in large saucepan over medium-high. Add bread pieces and 1 tsp (5 mL) thyme. Cook until bread is golden on both sides, turning with tongs, about 2 minutes total. Transfer croutons to bowl; sprinkle with salt and pepper.

Add remaining 4 Tbsp (60 mL) oil, garlic and crushed red pepper to same saucepan. Sauté over medium heat until fragrant, about 30 seconds. Add kale and stock, and bring to a boil. Reduce heat to medium-low, cover and simmer until kale wilts, about 5 minutes. Add tomatoes with juice, beans and 1 Tbsp (15 mL) thyme. Cover and simmer 15 minutes. Season with salt and pepper. Ladle ragout into shallow bowls. Top with croutons and serve.

1 serving: 420 Calories; 23 g Total Fat (17 g Mono, 2.5 g Poly, 3.5 g Sat); 0 mg Cholesterol; 46 g Carbohydrate (10 g Fibre, 2 g Sugar); 14 g Protein; 910 mg Sodium

Homemade Vegetable Stock

Makes 10 cups (2.5 L)

Heat oil in a large saucepan over medium. Add onions and cook, stirring, until softened. Add remaining ingredients. Bring to a boil over medium-high heat. Reduce heat and cook just below a simmer for 40 minutes, stirring occasionally. Remove from heat. Strain through a colander. Discard solids. Strain again through a cheesecloth-lined sieve. Discard solids. Season lightly with salt. If not using immediately, cool, uncovered, to room temperature, then chill, covered. Keep covered in refrigerator for up to 3 days, or freeze for up to 3 months.

1 cup (250 mL): 25 Calories; 2 g Total Fat (0 g Mono, 1.5 g Poly, 0 g Sat); 0 mg Cholesterol; 1 g Carbohydrate (0 g Fibre, 0 g Sugar); 0 g Protein; 5 mg Sodium

Tip

Potato peelings, mushrooms, fennel, turnip—anything you have on hand—will add nuances of flavour to this basic stock.

1 1/2 Tbsp (22 mL) grape seed oil

2 medium yellow onions, chopped

4 stalks celery, coarsely chopped

2 to 4 cups (500 mL to 1 L) vegetables and trimmings (see Tip)

2 medium carrots, coarsely chopped

1 bay leaf

1/4 cup (60 mL) coarsely chopped flat-leaf parsley

3 sprigs of fresh thyme

1/2 tsp (2 mL) whole black peppercorns

10 cups (2.5 L) water

salt to taste

Bread Stuffing with Caramelized Onion, Bacon and Apple

Serves 10

For many people, the star of the holiday meal is not the bird, but the stuffing. Leftovers, if there are any, are lovingly packed up and taken home to be eaten for a midnight snack, drizzled with precious drops of leftover gravy, or for breakfast, or with turkey in a sandwich. We didn't want to mess too much with a good thing, but the addition of caramelized onion and apples takes this stuffing one step further.

8 oz (225 g) bacon, cut into 1 inch (2.5 cm) pieces

10 cups (2.5 L) dried bread cubes

1 lb (454 g) yellow onions, cut into 1/2 inch (12 mm) dice

2 Gala apples, cored and cut into 1/2 inch (12 mm) dice

3 celery stalks, chopped

1/2 cup (125 mL) chopped fresh flat-leaf parsley

1 Tbsp (15 mL) chopped fresh thyme

1 Tbsp (15 mL) chopped fresh sage

1 tsp (5 mL) salt

freshly ground pepper to taste

3 eggs, lightly beaten

4 cups (1 L) chicken broth

Preheat oven to 350°F (175°C). In a medium sauté pan, cook bacon over medium heat until crisp. Drain bacon pieces on paper towel. Leave 2 Tbsp (30 mL) bacon fat in pan, and reserve the rest. Combine bacon with bread cubes in a large bowl. Add onions to pan and sauté over medium heat until golden, about 10 minutes. Add 2 Tbsp (30 mL) bacon fat and melt. Add apples and celery, and sauté, stirring frequently, until softened, about 5 minutes. Add parsley, thyme and sage, and season with salt and pepper. Cook, stirring, 1 minute more. Add to bread cubes and stir to combine. Add beaten eggs and broth. Mix well. Transfer to buttered deep baking dish. Bake, uncovered, until top is browned and crisp, about 1 hour.

1 serving: 260 Calories; 14 g Total Fat (6 g Mono, 2 g Poly, 4.5 g Sat); 90 mg Cholesterol; 25 g Carbohydrate (4 g Fibre, 0 g Sugar); 0 g Protein; 890 mg Sodium

We call it stuffing, but you could call it dressing instead since it's not actually stuffed inside the bird. Grandma might prefer the bird stuffed, but many cooking authorities today advise cooking the bird and the stuffing separately for many reasons, foremost of which is that for the stuffing to reach the required temperature, the bird is often over cooked.

Sausage and Chestnut Stuffing with Figs

Serves 6

When American chestnut trees grew abundantly in southern Ontario, chestnuts were incorporated into many dishes, chestnut stuffing being one of the most popular. Combined here with mild Italian sausage and dried figs, this stuffing is a delightful departure from the usual bread stuffing. Stuffing lovers might even be happy to have both kinds in one meal.

8 oz (225 g) mild Italian sausages, casings removed

3 large shallots, chopped

2 celery stalks, chopped

6 oz (170 g) dried figs, chopped

1 cup (250 mL) chicken broth, *divided*

3 Tbsp (45 mL) brandy

1/2 tsp (2 mL) dried thyme

4 cups (4 L) very coarsely ground fresh breadcrumbs

1 1/2 cups (375 mL) peeled, roasted chestnuts (see p. 67) or canned chestnuts (about 8 oz, 225 g), coarsely chopped

salt and freshly ground pepper to taste

Preheat oven to 350°F (175°C). Butter 8 x 8 x 2 inch (20 x 20 x 5 cm) glass baking dish. Sauté sausage in a large sauté pan over medium-high heat, breaking into small pieces with the back of a fork, until brown and cooked through, about 5 minutes. Add shallots and celery to pan, and sauté 5 minutes. Stir in figs, 1/2 cup (125 mL) chicken broth, brandy and thyme and bring to boil. Reduce heat, cover and simmer until figs are tender, about 5 minutes.

Mix breadcrumbs, chestnuts and sausage mixture in a large bowl. Stir in remaining 1/2 cup (125 mL) chicken broth. Season to taste with salt and pepper. Transfer stuffing to prepared baking dish. Cover baking dish with foil and bake for 25 minutes. Remove foil; bake stuffing until top begins to brown, about 10 more minutes.

1 serving: 620 Calories; 16 g Total Fat (6 g Mono, 3.5 g Poly, 5 g Sat); 25 mg Cholesterol; 93 g Carbohydrate (8 g Fibre, 23 g Sugar); 20 g Protein; 1240 mg Sodium

Mushroom Soufflés

Serves 9

With earthy flavour in a light, airy package, these soufflés are a mushroom-lover's dream. Don't be daunted by the idea of making soufflé—yes, they'll fall, but there's no need to worry about it—it's inevitable, and will happen to every soufflé, no matter the chef. The most important thing for success in soufflés is to not open the oven door while they're cooking. Serve immediately for maximum impact.

3 Tbsp (45 mL) butter

8 oz (225 g) mushrooms, finely chopped (use whatever is available, or a combination)

2 Tbsp (30 mL) chopped fresh thyme

1/2 tsp (2 mL) salt

3 Tbsp (45 mL) flour

1/2 cup (125 mL) milk (2 percent)

5 eggs, separated

1/3 cup (75 mL) grated Romano cheese

4 oz (113 g) soft goat cheese

Preheat oven to 350°F (175°C). In a medium saucepan, melt butter over medium heat. Add mushrooms, thyme and salt, and cook until tender. Stir in flour and cook, stirring constantly, about 1 minute. Gradually whisk in milk. Cook, stirring, until smooth, thickened and bubbling, about 2 minutes. Remove from heat and stir in egg yolks one at a time. Stir in Romano and goat cheeses. Set aside.

In a medium bowl, beat egg whites until stiff but not dry. Add 1/3 of the egg whites to mushroom mixture and stir to combine. (This process lightens the sauce so it will fold into egg whites easier.) Add lightened sauce to egg whites and fold in until mixed.

Spray individual 1 cup (250 mL) ramekins with non-stick cooking spray. Divide mixture among ramekins and arrange them on a baking sheet. Place on centre rack in oven and bake 25 to 30 minutes. Serve immediately; soufflés will hold their height for only a few minutes.

1 serving: 160 Calories; 11 g Total Fat (3 g Mono, 0.5 g Poly, 6 g Sat); 140 mg Cholesterol; 5 g Carbohydrate (trace Fibre, 2 g Sugar); 10 g Protein; 340 mg Sodium

Caramelized Fennel and Onion Mashed Potatoes

Serves 9

Creamy, perfectly smooth mashed potatoes are wonderfully delicious, but when you want something that's still comforting, but just a little different, it's time to play with your mashed potatoes. Caramelized fennel and onion add layers to both flavour and texture, while still maintaining the character of the original mashed potato.

3 lbs (1.4 kg) starchy potatoes such as Russets, peeled and cut into 2 inch (5 cm) chunks

1/2 cup (125 mL) butter, _divided_

1 bulb fennel, thinly sliced

1 medium white onion, cut into 1/2 inch (12 mm) dice

1/4 cup (60 mL) milk (2 percent)

1 tsp (5 mL) salt

1 Tbsp (30 mL) freshly ground pepper

Cook potatoes in a large pot of salted water until tender, about 20 minutes.

While potatoes cook, melt 1/4 cup (60 mL) butter in a large, deep sauté pan (if you only have shallow pans, use a saucepan instead) over medium-low heat. Add fennel and onions. Cook, stirring occasionally, until golden brown. Be careful not to let them burn.

Drain potatoes in a colander and let sit for 10 minutes to steam dry. Transfer to a large bowl and mash with a potato masher or pass through a ricer. In a small bowl or glass measuring cup, combine remaining butter with milk, and heat briefly in microwave until butter is melted and milk is warm. Season with salt and pepper. Stir into potatoes until just incorporated. Add fennel and onions, and stir again just until evenly distributed. Transfer to a serving dish and serve immediately.

**1 serving**: 210 Calories; 11 g Total Fat (2.5 g Mono, 0.5 g Poly, 7 g Sat); 30 mg Cholesterol; 25 g Carbohydrate (4 g Fibre, 2 g Sugar); 4 g Protein; 380 mg Sodium

Tip

Do not stir the potatoes too much or they will turn out gummy.

Tip

Fennel bulb looks somewhat like celery. In this recipe, cut the fronds off the stems; use the fronds as an anise-like flavour in salads or dressings, and discard the stems. Cut the root end off the bulb, then quarter the bulb and slice the quarters thinly.

Wild and White Rice Pilaf with Dried Cranberries

Serves 5

Canada harvests the biggest crop of truly wild (as opposed to farmed) wild rice, about 3.5 million pounds (1.58 million kg) a year. This grass is one of the most ancient grains known to man, with evidence of its growth in North America going back 12,000 years. Like other ancient grains, wild rice is a nutritional powerhouse, high in proteins, B vitamins and folic acid.

2 Tbsp (30 mL) butter

1/3 cup (75 mL) cipolline onions, julienned

1 cup (250 mL) wild and white rice blend

1/2 cup (125 mL) dried cranberries

1 Tbsp (15 mL) chopped fresh sage

1/2 tsp (2 mL) salt

2 cups (500 mL) water or broth

Preheat oven to 350°F (175°C). Melt butter in a medium ovenproof saucepan on low heat. Add onions and sauté until softened, 1 to 2 minutes. Add rice. Cook, stirring, until the grains of white rice become translucent, about 3 to 5 minutes. Add dried cranberries, sage and salt. Sauté 1 minute more. Add water or broth. Increase heat to medium-high and bring to a boil. Stir. Cover and transfer saucepan to oven. Cook for 45 minutes. Remove from oven. Fluff with a fork before serving.

1 serving: 210 Calories; 5 g Total Fat (1.5 g Mono, 0 g Poly, 3 g Sat); 10 mg Cholesterol; 37 g Carbohydrate (2 g Fibre, 9 g Sugar); 4 g Protein; 400 mg Sodium

Cipolline onions are an Italian variety of pearl onion (cipolline means "small onion" in Italian). Recognizable by their flat shape, they have a richer, sweeter flavour than other pearl onions.

Wild Mushroom Perogies

Serves 9

Whether you call them perogy, pyrohy or varenyky, these tasty little pastries have become a cold-weather staple across Canada, but especially in the Prairie provinces. The village of Glendon, Alberta, northeast of Edmonton, has even built a monument to these eastern European stuffed dumplings, with the world's biggest perogy standing 25 feet (7.5 m) tall. Perogies are most often filled with a mixture of mashed potato and cheese, but ours are more decadently filled with wild mushrooms. Serve with sour cream.

6 Tbsp (90 mL) butter

3 cups (750 mL) chopped wild mushrooms

1/3 cup (75 mL) finely chopped yellow onion

2 egg yolks, _divided_

1 Tbsp (15 mL) chopped fresh dill

2 tsp (10 mL) salt, plus more to taste

freshly ground pepper to taste

4 1/2 cups (1.1 L) all-purpose flour

2 cups (500 mL) sour cream

2 eggs

2 Tbsp (30 mL) olive oil

1 medium onion, cut into 1/2 inch (12 mm) dice

For the filling, melt 2 Tbsp (30 mL) butter in a large sauté pan over medium heat. Add mushrooms and onion. Cook, stirring, until mushrooms are tender and liquid has evaporated, about 7 to 9 minutes. Remove from heat. Add 1 egg yolk and dill, and season with salt and pepper. Stir to combine. Set aside.

For the dough, stir together flour and 2 tsp (10 mL) salt in a large bowl. Melt 2 Tbsp (30 mL) butter and combine with sour cream, eggs, 1 egg yolk and oil. In a second bowl, add wet ingredients to dry. Stir until well combined. Cover with damp kitchen towel and let stand 15 to 20 minutes.

To assemble, divide dough into 3 roughly equal portions. On lightly floured work surface, roll out 1 portion of dough to 1/16 inch (15 mm) thick. Keep remaining dough covered. Use a 3 inch (7.5 cm) round cutter to cut as many rounds in dough as will fit. Place 1 tsp (5 mL) filling on one half of each round. Lightly moisten the other half of each round with water. Fold over other half. Lightly pinch edges together to seal. Transfer to cloth-lined baking sheet. Repeat with remaining dough and filling. Leftover dough may be re-rolled once. (Perogies may be made up to this point then frozen on baking sheets before transferring to freezer bags to keep for up to 1 month.)

To cook, bring large pot of salted water to boil over medium-high heat. Cook perogies, in batches, stirring gently to prevent sticking, until they float to the surface, about 1 to 2 minutes. Use a slotted spoon to transfer to colander to drain.

Melt 2 Tbsp (30 mL) butter in a large sauté pan over medium heat. Add onion. Cook, stirring, until softened and almost golden, about 5 minutes. Add perogies. Stir to coat and warm through and serve.

1 serving: 470 Calories; 24 g Total Fat (8 g Mono, 1.5 g Poly, 13 g Sat); 135 mg Cholesterol; 53 g Carbohydrate (2 g Fibre, 1 g Sugar); 11 g Protein; 690 mg Sodium

Pumpkin Ravioli in Cider Broth

Serves 6

For many of us, pasta is the ultimate comfort food—soft, warm and pleasantly filling. Fresh, homemade pasta is even better than store bought. It's more flavourful and more tender, and can be filled with whatever you like. But making the dough can be time-consuming and requires special equipment. Fresh or frozen potsticker wrappers are a quick substitute for homemade dough.

3/4 cup (175 mL) pumpkin purée (see p. 135)

1 cup (250 mL) Ricotta cheese

1/4 cup (60 mL) grated Parmesan cheese (see Tip)

2 Tbsp (30 mL) chopped fresh sage

1/2 tsp (2 mL) chopped fresh thyme

salt and freshly ground pepper to taste

64 potsticker wrappers

2 Tbsp (30 mL) butter

1/3 cup (75 mL) minced shallots

1 1/2 cups (375 mL) chicken broth

1/2 cup (125 mL) apple cider

1 Tbsp (30 mL) chopped fresh parsley

shaved Parmiggiano-Reggiano cheese, for garnish

In a medium bowl, combine pumpkin purée, Ricotta, grated Parmesan, sage and thyme. Season with salt and pepper.

Place 8 wrappers on a work surface. Place 1 level Tbsp (15 mL) filling in centre of each. Brush edges with water and top with a second wrapper, pressing edges to seal. Repeat with remaining wrappers.

Melt butter in a large sauté pan over medium heat. Add shallots. Sauté until fragrant, about 1 minute. Increase heat to medium-high. Add broth and cider. Bring to a boil. Reduce heat and simmer 8 minutes. Add parsley, and season with salt and pepper.

Working in batches, cook ravioli in a pot of boiling salted water until just tender, about 1 minute. Using a slotted spoon, divide ravioli among shallow soup bowls. Bring cider broth to a simmer; ladle over ravioli. Top with shaved Parmiggiano-Reggiano.

1 serving: 260 Calories; 10 g Total Fat (2.5 g Mono, 0 g Poly, 6 g Sat); 50 mg Cholesterol; 31 g Carbohydrate (3 g Fibre, 5 g Sugar); 13 g Protein; 760 mg Sodium

Tip

When a recipe calls for grated Parmesan cheese, please do not use the powdered variety often sold in a large green shaker or a small bag. The bags or tubs of grated parmesan are acceptable to use if you're in a hurry, but a small block of Parmesan that you grate as needed will always be superior in flavour and texture, and it will stay fresh longer.

Spaghetti Squash with Pumpkin Seed Pesto

Serves 6

You'll understand where the spaghetti squash gets its name when you see the mound of spaghetti-like strands the flesh produces when cooked. Lighter and a little crisper than its namesake, but milder in flavour than most other squash, it makes a great foil for all sorts of sauces. Here we've paired it with a pumpkin seed pesto, but it's also great with a more traditional tomato sauce.

1 small spaghetti squash

2 Tbsp (30 mL) plus 2 tsp (10 mL) grape seed oil, *divided*

3/4 cup (175 mL) shelled pumpkin seeds (not toasted), *divided*

1/2 cup (125 mL) cilantro, lightly packed

1 1/2 tsp (7 mL) fresh lemon juice

1/4 tsp (1 mL) *each* salt and freshly ground pepper

Preheat oven to 350°F (175°C). Cut squash in half lengthwise. Scrape out seeds and pulp. Rub squash with 2 tsp (10 mL) grape seed oil. Place, skin side up, on baking sheet and bake 30 to 40 minutes until tender-crisp when pierced with a fork.

Heat 1 Tbsp (15 mL) oil in large sauté pan over medium-high. Add pumpkin seeds and toast, stirring often, until seeds begin to brown and puff up, about 2 to 4 minutes. Transfer to plate and cool completely.

For the pesto, combine 1/2 cup (125 mL) toasted pumpkin seeds with cilantro, lemon juice, salt and pepper in food processor. Pulse mixture and drizzle in remaining 1 Tbsp (15 mL) grape seed oil. Continue to pulse until ingredients come together in a coarse paste.

Draw a fork lengthwise through flesh of squash to separate strands. Toss squash strands with pesto. Sprinkle with remaining pumpkin seeds. Serve immediately.

1 serving: 120 Calories; 7 g Total Fat (1.5 g Mono, 4.5 g Poly, 1 g Sat); 0 mg Cholesterol; 11 g Carbohydrate (2 g Fibre, 0 g Sugar); 0 g Protein; 125 mg Sodium

 Pumpkin seeds may be small but they pack a nutritional punch. These little seeds support the immune system, lower "bad" (LDL) cholesterol and raise "good" (HDL) cholesterol levels, and stabilize blood sugar levels. They also have anti-inflammatory properties and are high in magnesium (which helps stabilize blood pressure), zinc (which supports the immune system and helps in cell growth and division) and antioxidants (which fight free-radicals and help protect against cancer). To get the maximum benefit from pumpkin seeds, they should be eaten raw, but you can also roast them at low temperatures, between 160 and 170°F (71 and 77°C) for up to 20 minutes. After 20 minutes, the fats are altered and lose some of their beneficial properties.

Squash and Wild Mushroom Risotto

Serves 4

Risotto is a traditional Italian dish that you'll find in many restaurants, and not just Italian ones. This method of cooking rice uses a special variety of rice called Arborio (Carnaroli or Vialone Nano can also be used) that is "toasted" or sautéed in olive oil or butter before the broth is added to the dish. It's not hard to make, but it does require love and care, because if you don't stir often enough, you'll taste the difference. If you stay close and stir often, you'll be rewarded with a very creamy rice that has a nice al dente bite.

4 cups (1 L) vegetable broth or chicken broth

2 Tbsp (30 mL) olive oil, *divided*

2 Tbsp (30 mL) butter, *divided*

1 cup (250 mL) winter squash, cut into 1/2 inch (12 mm) dice

6 oz (170 g) fresh wild mushrooms

salt and freshly ground black pepper to taste

1 small onion, finely chopped

1 clove of garlic, minced

1 cup (250 mL) Arborio or Carnaroli rice

1/2 cup (125 mL) dry white wine

1/3 cup (75 mL) grated Parmesan

In a medium saucepan, bring broth nearly to a boil, then reduce heat to low to keep warm.

In a large sauté pan, heat 1 Tbsp (15 mL) olive oil and 1 Tbsp (15 mL) butter over medium-low. Add squash and cook until lightly browned, about 5 minutes. Add mushrooms and cook until squash and mushrooms are tender, 3 to 5 minutes. Season to taste with salt and pepper and set aside.

In a large, heavy-bottomed saucepan, heat remaining olive oil and butter over medium-low. Add onion and cook until softened, about 3 minutes. Add garlic and cook another minute more. Add rice and cook, stirring constantly, until the grains of rice are mostly translucent but with an opaque centre, about 3 minutes. Increase heat to medium and add wine, stirring until wine is almost completely absorbed.

Add a ladle of broth (about 1/2 to 3/4 cup, 125 to 175 mL) and stir until almost completely absorbed. Continue adding broth by ladlefuls and cook, stirring constantly, until it is absorbed before adding another ladle of broth. After about 15 minutes, begin tasting the risotto before adding each new ladle of broth. When the rice is nearly done, firm but not crunchy, add another ladleful of broth, along with the squash and mushrooms. Continue stirring, and when the broth has been absorbed, the rice should be al dente. Stir in a little more broth along with the Parmesan, then season with salt and pepper. Serve immediately.

1 serving: 370 Calories; 15 g Total Fat (7 g Mono, 1 g Poly, 6 g Sat); 25 mg Cholesterol; 46 g Carbohydrate (2 g Fibre, 3 g Sugar); 8 g Protein; 1040 mg Sodium

Marinated Brussels Sprouts with Hazelnuts and Pomegranate

Serves 8

Roasting Brussels sprouts gives them an unexpected, nutty sweetness, and once you've tried them using this method you might never cook them any other way. The pomegranate marinade adds a tangy contrast to the caramelized sprouts. Look for pomegranate molasses at Middle Eastern grocers.

2 Tbsp (30 mL) grape seed oil

2 Tbsp (30 mL) pomegranate molasses

2 Tbsp (30 mL) chopped fresh oregano

1/4 tsp (1 mL) *each* salt and freshly ground pepper

2 lbs (900 g) Brussels sprouts, trimmed and cut in half lengthwise

1/4 cup (60 mL) pomegranate seeds

1/4 cup (60 mL) toasted sliced hazelnuts

Combine oil, pomegranate molasses, oregano, salt and pepper in a small bowl. Mix well. Place Brussels sprouts in a large bowl. Drizzle with marinade and toss to coat. Chill for 30 minutes.

Preheat oven to 350°F (175°C). Arrange sprouts cut side down in a large, shallow baking pan. Roast, without turning, until tender, about 45 minutes. Toss with pomegranate seeds and hazelnuts. Transfer to a serving dish.

1 serving: 130 Calories; 6 g Total Fat (2.5 g Mono, 3 g Poly, 0 g Sat); 0 mg Cholesterol; 17 g Carbohydrate (5 g Fibre, 7 g Sugar); 4 g Protein; 110 mg Sodium

Pomegranates add colour, texture and a burst of tart flavour to dishes from salads and soups to entrées and desserts. But prying the jewel-like seeds (or rather arils, which includes the pulp surrounding the seed) out of the fruit can be tortuous. It doesn't have to be. Cut the blossom end off, taking a little pith with it. Score the skin in quarters and break, but don't cut along the lines. Submerge pieces in a bowl of water, peel back the rind and pull out the seeds. The white pith will float, and the seeds will sink.

Succotash

Serves 5

Succotash in its most basic form pairs two First Nations peoples' staples: corn and beans. We've used soybeans and added some more of autumn's bounty to round out the dish: mushrooms, peppers and spinach. If you have semi-repressed memories of succotash as a mess of overcooked, slimy vegetables, don't run from this recipe. Our freshly made version will be a happy surprise.

2 slices bacon, cut crosswise into very thin strips

1 Tbsp (15 mL) butter

2 cups (500 mL) fresh corn kernels (from 3 to 4 ears)

2 cups (500 mL) shelled edamame

1 cup (250 mL) sliced or torn fresh mushrooms

1/2 cup (125 mL) diced red bell pepper

3/4 cup (175 mL) whipping cream (30 percent)

1/4 cup (60 mL) water

1/2 tsp (2 mL) *each* salt and freshly ground black pepper

2 cups (500 mL) baby spinach leaves

1 bunch of green onions, thinly sliced

Cook bacon in a heavy skillet over moderate heat, stirring frequently, until crisp, about 5 minutes. Transfer bacon with a slotted spoon to paper towels to drain, then add butter to bacon fat in skillet and melt over moderate heat. Add corn, edamame, mushrooms and pepper, and cook, stirring, for 2 minutes. Add cream, water, salt and pepper, then simmer, partially covered, until vegetables are tender, 10 to 15 minutes. Stir in bacon, spinach and green onions. Cook until spinach begins to wilt. Season with salt and pepper. Serve immediately.

1 serving: 350 Calories; 24 g Total Fat (7 g Mono, 1.5 g Poly, 11 g Sat); 60 mg Cholesterol; 24 g Carbohydrate (5 g Fibre, 4 g Sugar); 12 g Protein; 420 mg Sodium

Edamame is a fancy name for soybeans. You can find them still in their pods in the frozen foods section of the grocery store; use them to make tasty and extremely nutritious snacks. They are also available shelled and frozen.

Roasted Root Vegetables with Maple Balsamic Glaze

Serves 5

Yes, we know, maple syrup is a spring ingredient, but it tastes like fall. Roasting root vegetables brings out their inherent sweetness, and the sweet and sour Maple Balsamic Glaze crisps the outsides of the vegetables for a play of textures, flavours and fall colours, all in one simple dish.

2 Tbsp (30 mL) balsamic vinegar

2 Tbsp (30 mL) grape seed oil

2 Tbsp (30 mL) maple syrup

1/2 tsp (2 mL) salt

1 tsp (5 mL) freshly ground pepper

3 large beets (golden or candy cane beets won't bleed and colour the other vegetables), peeled and cut into 1 inch (2.5 cm) pieces

3 large carrots, peeled and cut into 1 inch (2.5 cm) pieces

3 large parsnips, peeled and cut into 1 inch (2.5 cm) pieces

1 large sweet potato, peeled and cut into 1 inch (2.5 cm) pieces

2 large white onions, cut into wedges

For the glaze, combine vinegar, oil, maple syrup, salt and pepper in a small bowl, and beat with a fork or small whisk until well combined. Set aside.

Preheat oven to 350°F (175°C). Combine vegetables in a large bowl. Drizzle with glaze. Toss to coat. Spread in a single layer on baking sheet. Roast until tender, about 45 minutes. Serve immediately.

1 serving: 230 Calories; 6 g Total Fat (1.5 g Mono, 4 g Poly, 0.5 g Sat); 0 mg Cholesterol; 44 g Carbohydrate (9 g Fibre, 18 g Sugar); 3 g Protein; 330 mg Sodium

The colourful and often-overlooked beet deserves a higher place in our vegetable choices. The deep, rich maroon of some of the oldest and most popular cultivars make it extremely important nutritionally, but modern varieties in oranges, pinks and candy-cane are available nowadays.

Carrot and Beet Latkes with Apple and Green Onion Salsa

Serves 8

Traditional latkes, made from potatoes, are delicious to begin with, but when made with carrots and beets, they pack a heavier nutritional punch and have new layers of flavour. The tart Apple and Green Onion Salsa is a great contrast to the crisp, slightly sweet latkes, but once you taste it, you'll find plenty of other dishes to pair it with.

3 cups (750 mL) peeled, coarsely grated beets (about 3 medium)

3 cups (750 mL) peeled, coarsely grated carrots

6 Tbsp (90 mL) all-purpose flour

3/4 tsp (4 mL) baking powder

2 Tbsp (30 mL) peeled, finely grated ginger root

1 1/2 tsp (7 mL) salt

1 1/2 tsp (7 mL) ground cumin

3/4 tsp (4 mL) ground coriander

1/4 tsp (1 mL) freshly ground black pepper

3 large eggs, beaten

grape seed oil, for frying

Place beets in a large bowl and press with paper towels to absorb any moisture. Repeat in a separate bowl with carrots. In another large bowl, mix flour, baking powder, ginger, salt, cumin, coriander and pepper. Mix in beets and carrots, then eggs.

Pour enough oil into a large sauté pan to cover bottom and place pan over medium heat. Working in batches, drop beet and carrot mixture in 1/4 cup (60 mL) portions into pan; spread to about 3 1/2 inch (9 cm) rounds. Fry until golden, about 5 minutes per side. Transfer latkes to baking sheet. Serve topped with Apple and Green Onion Salsa.

3 latkes with 1/2 cup (125 mL) salsa: 200 Calories; 8 g Total Fat (2 g Mono, 4 g Poly, 1 g Sat); 80 mg Cholesterol; 31 g Carbohydrate (5 g Fibre, 18 g Sugar); 5 g Protein; 630 mg Sodium

Tip

Latkes can be made up to 6 hours ahead. Let stand at room temperature. Warm in 350°F (175°C) oven until crisp, about 10 minutes.

Apple and Green Onion Salsa
Makes 5 cups (1.25 L)

Coarsely grate apples into a strainer set over a large bowl. Press and turn apples to drain off excess juices. Transfer apples to a medium bowl. Stir in green onions and chilies. Whisk lemon juice, honey and lemon peel in a small bowl and mix into apples. Season with salt and pepper. Salsa can be made 6 hours ahead. Cover and chill until ready to serve.

1/2 cup (125 mL): 60 Calories; 0 g Total Fat (0 g Mono, 0 g Poly, 0 g Sat); 0 mg Cholesterol; 16 g Carbohydrate (2 g Fibre, 12 g Sugar); trace Protein; 60 mg Sodium

1 1/2 lbs (680 g) Fuji apples (about 3 large), peeled, halved and cored

1/2 cup (125 mL) minced green onions

2 Tbsp (30 mL) seeded, minced jalapeño chilies (see Introduction)

1/2 cup (125 mL) fresh lemon juice

3 Tbsp (45 mL) honey

4 tsp (20 mL) packed, finely grated lemon peel

salt and freshly ground pepper to taste

Turnip and Apple Gratin

Serves 6

Turnips are certainly not the most popular vegetable around, but you might begin to wonder why after you taste this recipe. We've taken the guilt out of gratin by using white wine instead of cream, and this dish comes out surprisingly light and delicate.

6 Tbsp (90 mL) butter

1/3 cup (75 mL) water

1/3 cup (75 mL) dry white wine

2 tsp (10 mL) sugar

1 1/2 lbs (680 g) medium turnips, trimmed but unpeeled, cut into 1/4 inch (6 mm) thick rounds

1 1/2 lbs (680 g) tart apples (such as Granny Smith, Pippin or Pink Lady), peeled, halved, cored and cut into 1/4 inch (6 mm) thick slices

2 tsp (10 mL) fine sea salt

1 Tbsp (30 mL) packed, chopped fresh thyme

Preheat oven to 400°F (200°C). Melt butter in a large non-stick saucepan over medium heat. Add water, wine and sugar. Bring to a boil. Cool to lukewarm.

Arrange turnips and apples in a buttered 12 inch (30 cm) casserole dish in alternating layers, sprinkling every other layer with salt and thyme. Cover dish with parchment paper, then cover with foil, shiny side down. Bake gratin until turnips are tender, about 55 minutes. Uncover and bake until top browns and juices bubble thickly, about 20 minutes longer. Let gratin stand 15 minutes before serving.

1 serving: 210 Calories; 12 g Total Fat (3 g Mono, 0.5 g Poly, 7 g Sat); 30 mg Cholesterol; 25 g Carbohydrate (5 g Fibre, 18 g Sugar); 1 g Protein; 870 mg Sodium

What's a turnip, what's a rutabaga, what's a swede... A turnip has white flesh and a reddish or purplish tinge on the skin. A rutabaga, which is a cross between a cabbage and a turnip, has yellow flesh and a more brownish exterior. The word "rutabaga" comes from a Swedish word, which is why some people call rutabagas "swedes." They are all in the brassica family of healthy vegetables.

Molasses Horseradish-glazed Sweet Potatoes

Serves 9

High in antioxidants, vitamins A, C and B6, sweet potatoes are a nutritional powerhouse. If you've grown tired of plain sweet potatoes in their many forms, this recipe may be just the thing for you. The combination of molasses and horseradish is more than the sum of its parts, transforming these sweet potatoes into something extraordinary.

3 lbs (1.4 kg) medium sweet potatoes, peeled and cut lengthwise into 8 spears each

1/4 cup (60 mL) grape seed oil

1 1/4 tsp (6 mL) salt, *divided*

5 Tbsp (75 mL) butter

1/3 cup (75 mL) molasses (not robust or blackstrap)

1/3 cup (75 mL) bottled horseradish including juice

Put oven rack in lower third of oven and preheat oven to 450°F (230°C). If potato spears are very long, halve them diagonally. In a large bowl, toss with oil and 3/4 tsp (4 mL) salt. Spread in a single layer in a large, shallow baking pan. Roast, turning once or twice, until tender, 18 to 22 minutes. (Sweet potatoes can be prepared up to this point up to 2 hours ahead).

While potatoes roast, combine butter, molasses, horseradish (with juice) and remaining 1/2 tsp (2 mL) salt in a small saucepan over medium-high heat. Bring to a boil, stirring, then reduce heat and simmer, stirring occasionally, until slightly thickened and reduced to about 3/4 cup (175 mL), about 5 minutes.

Transfer mixture to a blender and purée for 30 seconds. Pour through a fine-mesh sieve into a heatproof bowl, pressing on and discarding solids. Drizzle glaze over cooked sweet potatoes and gently toss until coated. Just before serving, bake glazed sweet potatoes in lower third of oven until hot, 3 to 5 minutes.

1 serving: 280 Calories; 13 g Total Fat (3 g Mono, 4.5 g Poly, 4.5 g Sat); 15 mg Cholesterol; 41 g Carbohydrate (5 g Fibre, 15 g Sugar); 3 g Protein; 500 mg Sodium

 Molasses is formed as white sugar is refined from sugarcane syrup. Although it may not look very tasty, its dark, caramelized flavour is an indispensable ingredient in gingerbread and other foods. Molasses comes in three varieties—light or mild, which can be served on pancakes and waffles, dark, which is often used in baking, and blackstrap, which is much thicker and more bitter. Blackstrap molasses has the highest concentration of vitamins, minerals and iron, and is often touted as a health food, but its bitter flavour makes it unsuitable for use in most recipes.

Sweet Potato and Parsnip Purée

Serves 4

This dish is so simple, but its gentle sweetness and silky texture are heavenly. The parsnips add an aromatic quality that the sweet potatoes alone wouldn't have. The sweetness of this recipe makes it a particularly good accompaniment for spicy dishes.

2 medium sweet potatoes, peeled and cut into 1/2 inch (12 mm) pieces

4 parsnips, peeled and sliced 1/4 inch (6 mm) thick

3 Tbsp (45 mL) butter

1/4 cup (60 mL) milk

3 Tbsp (45 mL) packed light brown sugar

1/2 tsp (2 mL) salt

freshly ground pepper to taste

1/4 cup (60 mL) toasted sliced hazelnuts

Bring a large saucepan of salted water to a boil. Add potatoes and parsnips and boil gently until tender, about 12 minutes. Drain well and transfer to a food processor.

Add butter and purée until smooth. Add milk, brown sugar and salt, and blend well. Season with pepper. Transfer to a serving dish and sprinkle with hazelnuts.

1 serving: 340 Calories; 14 g Total Fat (6 g Mono, 1 g Poly, 6 g Sat); 25 mg Cholesterol; 52 g Carbohydrate (10 g Fibre, 21 g Sugar); 5 g Protein; 420 mg Sodium

Tip

To toast nuts, preheat oven to 350°F (175°C). Lay nuts in a single layer on a rimmed baking sheet. Cook sliced nuts about 5 to 8 minutes, whole nuts about 8 to 12 minutes, stirring once or twice while cooking. Smaller quantities of nuts can be toasted in a dry pan over medium-low heat, stirring often to ensure they don't burn.

Carrot, Parsnip and Hazelnut Gratin

Serves 9

Potatoes aren't the only vegetables that benefit from the creamy treatment of a gratin. Here, carrots and parsnips seek comfort from the cold autumn earth by wrapping themselves in a warm blanket of lightly spiced cream layered with crunchy hazelnuts. You may have trouble deciding whether it's dinner or dessert.

1 lb (454 g) carrots, peeled

1 lb (454 g) parsnips, peeled

1/2 cup (125 mL) toasted sliced hazelnuts, *divided*

2 cups (500 mL) whipping cream (30 percent)

1 cup (250 mL) chicken broth

1 tsp (5 mL) cinnamon

1/4 tsp (1 mL) nutmeg

1 1/2 tsp (7 mL) salt

1 tsp (5 mL) freshly ground pepper

Preheat oven to 400°F (200°C). Use a mandolin to cut carrots lengthwise into thin ribbons. Repeat with parsnips. Reserve 2 Tbsp (30 mL) hazelnuts. In a 2 quart (2 L) baking dish, lay down a layer of carrot strips, sprinkle with hazelnuts, lay down a layer of parsnip strips, sprinkle with hazelnuts, and repeat until almost all carrots and parsnips are used up. For last layer, alternate carrot and parsnip strips in basket-weave pattern.

In a medium bowl, combine whipping cream, broth, cinnamon, nutmeg, salt and pepper. Mix well. Pour over parsnips and carrots.

Bake gratin for 30 minutes. Press down on parsnips and carrots to moisten evenly. Continue baking until veggies are tender and liquid is thickened and bubbling, about 35 minutes more. Remove from oven and let stand 10 minutes. Sprinkle with reserved hazelnuts and serve.

1 serving: 260 Calories; 21 g Total Fat (8 g Mono, 1 g Poly, 11 g Sat); 60 mg Cholesterol; 17 g Carbohydrate (5 g Fibre, 5 g Sugar); 3 g Protein; 380 mg Sodium

Potato-crusted Mushroom and Spinach Frittata

Serves 6

This frittata actually falls somewhere between frittata and quiche with a crispy, savoury potato crust. Warm and comforting, this comes close to being a perfect food, suitable for breakfast, lunch or dinner.

2 tsp (10 mL) grape seed oil

1 cup (250 mL) chopped mixed mushrooms

2 cups (500 mL) lightly packed spinach leaves

1/2 lb (225 g) yellow-fleshed potatoes, peeled

7 eggs, *divided*

2 Tbsp (30 mL) all-purpose flour

1 tsp (5 mL) fresh lemon juice

salt and freshly ground pepper, to taste

grape seed oil, for frying

1/2 cup (125 mL) cream or milk

1/4 cup (60 mL) grated Romano cheese

Heat oil in a medium sauté pan over medium. Stir in mushrooms. Cook, stirring occasionally until tender and light golden. Add spinach and cook until just wilted, about 1 minute more. Remove from heat and set aside.

Preheat broiler to 500°F (260°C). Using the largest holes on a box grater, grate potato into a large bowl. Mix in 1 egg, flour, lemon juice, salt and pepper. Transfer mixture to a fine-mesh sieve set over the same bowl.

Add oil to medium ovenproof sauté pan until it is 1/4 inch (6 mm) deep. Heat over medium-high. Spread potato batter to cover bottom of pan, pressing with the back of a spoon. Fry until golden brown on bottom, about 4 minutes. Using a long spatula, carefully flip mixture over.

Spread cooked mushrooms and spinach overtop. Whisk 6 eggs, cream, salt and pepper in a medium bowl to combine. Pour over mixture in pan. Sprinkle with cheese. Cook until eggs are almost set, about 5 to 6 minutes. Remove from heat and place under broiler to finish cooking until set and golden on top, about 1 or 2 minutes. Serve immediately.

1 serving: 160 Calories; 10 g Total Fat (2.5 g Mono, 3 g Poly, 3.5 g Sat); 50 mg Cholesterol; 13 g Carbohydrate (2 g Fibre, 0 g Sugar); 6 g Protein; 620 mg Sodium

Spinach is a popular ingredient in the cuisines of many different regions. However, this healthy green is actually native to central and southwestern Asia. There are three main types of spinach including savoy, which has crinkly, dark green leaves. Flat leaf spinach is perhaps the most common variety and has broad, flat leaves. Semi-savoy is a hybrid variety with less crinkly leaves than savoy spinach, which makes it easier to clean. Spinach is rich in vitamins, minerals and is said to be a powerful antioxidant. Although we're not sure that spinach will give you super-strength, we are sure it's good for you!

Butternut Squash with Wilted Greens and Pancetta

Serves 4

This dish has it all—sweet from the squash, salty from the pancetta and a little bite from the greens. And, as a bonus, it's good for you (or mostly good for you because you won't be able to resist a second helping).

8 oz (225 g) chopped pancetta

1 medium sweet onion, diced

1 small butternut squash, seeded, peeled and diced into 3/4 inch (2 cm) pieces

3 cloves garlic, minced

2 cups (500 mL) chicken broth

1 bunch or 2 cups (500 mL) quick-cooking greens, such as mizuna, arugula or spinach

salt and freshly ground pepper to taste

1/4 cup (60 mL) grated or shaved Asiago cheese

Cook pancetta in a large sauté pan over medium heat until crispy. Remove from pan, drain on paper towels, and set aside.

In same pan, cook onion in pancetta drippings over medium-low heat, stirring occasionally, until softened. Increase heat to medium and add squash. Cook, stirring occasionally, until lightly browned, about 5 minutes. Add garlic and cook until fragrant, about 1 minute. Pour in chicken broth and bring to a simmer. Cover and cook until squash is nearly tender, about 10 minutes. Uncover and continue to cook until most of the liquid has evaporated and the squash is tender, about 10 minutes more. Stir in greens and cook until greens are tender and beginning to wilt, 2 to 3 minutes. Season with salt and pepper. Stir in Asiago and pancetta. Serve immediately.

1 serving: 340 Calories; 20 g Total Fat (0.5 g Mono, 0 g Poly, 7 g Sat); 55 mg Cholesterol; 27 g Carbohydrate (4 g Fibre, 6 g Sugar); 16 g Protein; 1750 mg Sodium

Look for pancetta—an Italian bacon—in the deli section of your grocery store. Chopped into cubes and fried, it adds a delicious salty bacon flavour to soups, stews, scrambled eggs—even sprinkled on Brussels sprouts!

Slow-cooked Kale

Serves 6

Kale loves cold weather and tastes especially good later in the autumn, because light frost brings out the sweetness in the leaves. If you think you don't like kale, you just haven't tried the right recipe. A quick braise makes it soft and tender, and sun-dried tomatoes and garlic add layers of flavour.

2 bunches of kale

2 Tbsp (30 mL) grape seed oil

1 shallot, minced

salt, to taste

3 large cloves garlic, minced

pinch of red chili flakes

1/4 cup (60 mL) chopped sun-dried tomatoes

2 tsp (10 mL) balsamic vinegar

1 tsp (5 mL) brown sugar

1/4 cup (60 mL) chicken broth, plus more as needed

freshly ground pepper to taste

1/4 cup (60 mL) grated Romano cheese

Strip kale leaves away from the thick stem. Discard stems. Wash leaves well to remove all grit. Shake water from them but don't worry about drying them well. Slice into long, thin (about 1/2 inch, 12 mm) strips. Heat oil in a large saucepan over medium-high. Sauté shallots until softened. Add a pinch of salt, then garlic and chili flakes. Mix well and cook for another minute.

Increase heat to high. Add greens with water still clinging to them. Add sun-dried tomatoes, vinegar, brown sugar and broth. Stir, cover and let greens cook down for 5 minutes. Stir, add more broth if greens are dry, cover and cook for 5 to 10 minutes more. Season with salt and pepper. Transfer to a serving dish. Sprinkle with Romano and serve.

1 serving: 140 Calories; 7 g Total Fat (1.5 g Mono, 4 g Poly, 1 g Sat); trace Cholesterol; 17 g Carbohydrate (3 g Fibre, 2 g Sugar); 7 g Protein; 430 mg Sodium

Use real Pecorino Romano cheese, a product of Italy, instead of the more commonly available Romano cheese made in North America, if you wish. Many European nations have laws that protect their historic agricultural products such as cheeses, and Pecorino Romano is protected by Italian law.

Fennel and Garlic Fondue

Serves 6

Here, "fondue" refers not to the melted cheese dish cooked in its own specialized pot, but to the melt-in-your-mouth tenderness of the fennel and garlic. Cooked slow and low, garlic loses its bite but doesn't become as sweet as when roasted, and fennel becomes a more mellow version of itself. This side is an ideal accompaniment for spicy or more strongly flavoured dishes.

3 Tbsp (45 mL) olive oil

2 bulbs of fennel, cores left on, thinly sliced

1 head of garlic, cloves separated and peeled

1/2 tsp (2 mL) salt

1 tsp (5 mL) pepper

fennel fronds for garnish

Heat oil in a deep sauté pan or large saucepan over medium-low. Add fennel, garlic, salt and pepper. Cook, stirring occasionally, until fennel and garlic are very tender, about 30 to 35 minutes. Transfer to a serving dish, garnish with fennel fronds and serve immediately.

1 serving: 100 Calories; 7 g Total Fat (4.5 g Mono, 0.5 g Poly, 1 g Sat); 0 mg Cholesterol; 9 g Carbohydrate (3 g Fibre, 0 g Sugar); 2 g Protein; 240 mg Sodium

Many people think of fennel as a tastier substitute for celery, best eaten raw. But cooking mellows it and makes the flavour more delicate. The shape of the bulb also affects flavour: squat, rounded bulbs are juicier, while flatter, elongated ones have richer flavour.

Braised Red Cabbage

Serves 8

The shift to cooler weather marks not only the beginning of autumn, but also braising season. Long, slow cooking with moist heat fills your kitchen with comforting aromas. Braising is most often used for cooking less tender cuts of meat, but it yields delicious results with vegetables too. Sweet and mildly spiced, this recipe is mulled apple cider reincarnated as cabbage. Its flavour improves the second and third days after you make it.

1 head of red cabbage, cut into 8 wedges

1/2 cup (125 mL) butter

2 cups (500 mL) dry red wine

2 cups (500 mL) water

1/2 cup (125 mL) apple cider vinegar

1 sweet apple, preferably Gala or Fuji, peeled and coarsely grated

1 1/2 Tbsp (22 mL) sugar

1 tsp (5 mL) salt

10 whole black peppercorns

2 whole cloves

1 bay leaf

salt and freshly ground pepper to taste

Slice each cabbage wedge crosswise into 1/4 inch (6 mm) thick slices. Heat butter in large saucepan over medium-high until foam subsides. Add cabbage. Cook, stirring frequently, until wilted and slightly browned, about 20 minutes. Add wine, water, vinegar, apple, sugar and salt. Bring to a boil.

Make a spice bundle by wrapping peppercorns, cloves and bay leaf in a piece of cheesecloth and tying with string. Add to saucepan. Reduce heat. Lay a round of parchment paper directly on top of cabbage in pot, then cover with lid. Simmer until cabbage is tender, about 2 hours.

Remove and discard spice bundle. Season with salt and pepper. Serve hot. Cabbage may be kept, covered and refrigerated, for up to 5 days.

1 serving: 210 Calories; 12 g Total Fat (3 g Mono, 0.5 g Poly, 7 g Sat); 30 mg Cholesterol; 15 g Carbohydrate (3 g Fibre, 10 g Sugar); 2 g Protein; 480 mg Sodium

Red cabbage has a taste similar to green cabbage but it bleeds a purplish red into other foods and is therefore not as popular as green cabbage. It is often braised, as in this recipe, but it can also be eaten raw in slaws and salads. Nutritionists like red cabbage because the chemicals that give it its colour also have many health benefits.

Wine-glazed Onions

Serves 8

Pearl onions, naturally sweeter than other onion varieties, often bring a little sweetness to fall stews and other braised dishes. In this side dish, glazed with red wine and honey, the onions play the starring role.

2 1/2 lbs (1.1 kg) pearl onions, blanched and peeled (see Tip)

1 1/2 cups (375 mL) red wine

2 Tbsp (30 mL) butter

2 Tbsp (30 mL) honey

2 sprigs of fresh thyme

1/2 tsp (2 mL) salt

1/4 tsp (1 mL) freshly ground black pepper

Heat a large sauté pan over medium-low. Add wine, butter, honey, thyme, salt and pepper. Stir until well combined. Add onions. Simmer, uncovered, stirring occasionally, until onions are tender and most of the liquid has evaporated, about 45 minutes.

1 serving: 160 Calories; 3 g Total Fat (0.5 g Mono, 0 g Poly, 2 g Sat); 10 mg Cholesterol; 25 g Carbohydrate (0 g Fibre, 9 g Sugar); 2 g Protein; 190 mg Sodium

Tip

To make pearl onions easier to peel, bring large pot of salted water to a boil. Blanch pearl onions for 1 minute. Drain, rinse under cold running water and peel.

Pearl onions are also known as tree onions or walking onions because the plants form bulblets at the top of their stalks, whereas other onions form flowers. In some varieties, these bulbs grow heavy enough to bend the stalk of the plant, and the bulbs plant themselves into the earth and continue their walk around the garden.

Pear Cranberry Compote

Serves 8

Sweet pears and sour cranberries lightly scented with rosemary make a surprising mix of sweet and savoury. Not sure what to eat it with? Neither were we, so we tried it with both dinner and dessert, and we still can't decide. It's great with desserts—try it alongside our Gingerbread Bread Puddings (p. 144) or over ice cream. And it's just as good with dinner—on top of poultry or pork.

6 Tbsp (90 mL) sugar

1/4 cup (60 mL) water

2 Bartlett pears, peeled, cored, and cut into 1 inch (2.5 cm) pieces

1 cup (250 mL) cranberries, fresh or frozen

2 Tbsp (30 mL) chopped fresh rosemary

Combine sugar and water in a medium saucepan over medium-low heat. Stir until sugar has completely dissolved. Add pears, cranberries and rosemary. Cover and simmer until pears are just tender, about 8 minutes. Serve warm.

1 serving: 80 Calories; 0 g Total Fat (0 g Mono, 0 g Poly, 0 g Sat); 0 mg Cholesterol; 20 g Carbohydrate (3 g Fibre, 16 g Sugar); 0 g Protein; 0 mg Sodium

Sassamanash, Ibimi, mossberry, bounceberry, cranberry. This native North American fruit with many names and many uses was long relegated to a single use as a jiggling, cylindrical side for the star of the holiday meal. Thanks to its newfound superfruit status, we are finally embracing the versatility of the cranberry. Many popular "new" uses have evolved from more traditional ones: dried cranberries were a common ingredient in pemmican, and early settlers enjoyed them in tarts and, of course, cranberry sauce.

Gingered Squash Relish

Makes 4 cups (1 L)

Squash is one of the world's oldest cultivated foods; *Apicius,* compiled in the late 4th or 5th century BC and considered to be the world's oldest cookbook, offers nine different recipes for squash. We've become accustomed to eating squash in both savoury and sweet dishes, but this relish is likely to be a pleasant surprise. Raw squash, lightly pickled, makes a delicious accompaniment to pork and poultry dishes, or adds extra zing to sandwiches of leftover turkey.

1/2 cup (125 mL) rice vinegar

1/2 tsp (2 mL) salt

2 Tbsp (30 mL) honey

2 Tbsp (30 mL) peeled and finely grated ginger root

1/4 tsp (1 mL) cayenne

2 lbs (900 g) buttercup squash, peeled, seeded and coarsely shredded

1 bunch of green onions, finely chopped

Stir together vinegar and salt in a large bowl until salt has dissolved. Add honey, ginger and cayenne, and stir until well blended. Add squash and green onion, and toss well. Cover and refrigerate, tossing occasionally, overnight or for up to 2 days to allow flavours to develop.

1/4 cup (60 mL): 40 Calories; 0 g Total Fat (0 g Mono, 0 g Poly, 0 g Sat); 0 mg Cholesterol; 10 g Carbohydrate (1 g Fibre, 4 g Sugar); trace Protein; 75 mg Sodium

Tip

For best flavour, choose squash carefully. So-called winter squashes are at their peak from late autumn and into winter, because their flavour improves with storage time. If you do buy squash close to when they are harvested, look for brightly coloured but not shiny rinds; later in the year, the colours may fade, but flavour will not be affected. They should be rock-solid; soft squash are past their prime, and if you can scrape off the skin or nick it with a fingernail, the squash is too young. Finally, look for squash with stems still attached, as bacteria can get into the squash where the stem has been removed.

Do not refrigerate winter squash until they have been cut open. Ideal storage temperature is between 50 and 60°F (10 and 15°C), but higher temperatures will not harm flavour, only shorten storage time. They'll last longer if you store them out of direct light, but we'll understand if you can't resist using them for home décor.

Sweet Potato Sourdough

Makes 2 loaves

If scent is strongly associated with memory, what could bring fonder memories to mind than the smell of homemade bread baking in the oven? With this recipe, that wonderfully evocative aroma will linger for two days, because you'll need to make the potato sourdough starter one day ahead.

1 x 9 to 11 oz (260 to 320 g) sweet potato, peeled and cut into 1 inch (2.5 cm) pieces

2 tsp (10 mL) dry yeast, *divided*

1/4 cup (60 mL) warm water (105 to 115°F, 41 to 46°C)

2 Tbsp (30 mL) unsalted butter, melted

1 Tbsp (15 mL) honey

1 tsp (5 mL) salt

2 cups (500 mL) whole wheat flour

2 1/4 cups (550 mL) unbleached all-purpose flour

1 large egg white, beaten

For the starter, cook sweet potato in water in medium saucepan until tender, about 15 minutes. Strain 1 1/2 cups (375 mL) cooking water into a large bowl (add more water if necessary to measure 1 1/2 cups, 375 mL). Cool liquid to 105 to 115°F (41 to 46°C). Mash sweet potato in a small bowl until smooth. Add mashed sweet potato and 1 tsp (5 mL) yeast to cooking liquid. Cover bowl with plastic wrap and let starter stand at room temperature overnight.

For sourdough, pour warm water into a small bowl. Sprinkle 1 tsp (5 mL) yeast over top and stir to blend. Let stand until yeast dissolves, about 10 minutes. Stir yeast mixture into starter. Stir in melted butter, honey and salt. Mix in whole wheat flour. Mix in enough all-purpose flour, 1/2 cup (125 mL) at a time, to form a soft dough. Turn dough out onto floured work surface. Knead until smooth and elastic, about 4 minutes. Form dough into a ball.

Butter a large bowl. Place dough in bowl; turn to coat. Cover with plastic. Let dough rise in a warm draft-free area until doubled in volume, about 1 hour. Lightly flour 2 large baking sheets. Punch down dough. Turn dough out onto floured work surface and knead until smooth, about 3 minutes. Divide dough in half. Roll each half between palms and work surface into 14 inch (36 cm) long loaf. Transfer to prepared baking sheets. Cover with dry towel. Let rise in warm draft-free area until almost doubled in volume, about 30 minutes.

Position 1 rack in centre and 1 rack in top third of oven and preheat oven to 500°F (260°C). Using a sharp knife, cut 5 diagonal slashes in surface of each loaf. Brush loaves with egg white and bake 10 minutes. Reduce oven temperature to 400°F (200°C). Bake about 15 minutes longer until loaves are brown and sound hollow when tapped on bottom, switching location of baking sheets and rotating them halfway through baking. Cool on racks.

1 slice: 100 Calories; 1.5 g Total Fat (0 g Mono, 0 g Poly, 0.5 g Sat); 10 mg Cholesterol; 19 g Carbohydrate (2 g Fibre, 1 g Sugar); 3 g Protein; 115 mg Sodium

Rosemary Black Pepper Cornbread

Makes 2 loaves

Cornbread is another product of the collaboration between First Nations people and early settlers: the combination of First Nations ingredients with European techniques produced this enduring favourite. Our version uses fresh sweet corn, along with some added bite from rosemary and black pepper, all rounded out with a little Parmesan cheese.

1 1/2 cups (375 mL) cornmeal

1/2 cup (125 mL) all-purpose flour

1 Tbsp (15 mL) sugar

2 tsp (10 mL) baking powder

1 tsp (5 mL) baking soda

1 tsp (5 mL) salt

2 eggs

1 1/2 cups (375 mL) buttermilk

1 1/2 cups (375 mL) corn kernels

1/2 cup (125 mL) grated Parmesan

2 Tbsp (30 mL) chopped fresh rosemary

1 Tbsp (15 mL) cracked black pepper

Preheat oven to 400°F (200°C). In a large bowl, sift together cornmeal, flour, sugar, baking powder, baking soda and salt. In another bowl, lightly beat eggs and buttermilk to combine. Add buttermilk mixture, corn, Parmesan, rosemary and pepper to cornmeal mixture. Mix until just combined. Pour into two 9 x 13 inch (23 x 33 cm) greased loaf pans. Bake for 25 minutes.

Serve with butter, warm or at room temperature. Keep in an airtight container at room temperature for up to 2 days.

1 slice: 80 Calories; 1.5 g Total Fat (0 g Mono, 0 g Poly, 0.5 g Sat); 20 mg Cholesterol; 13 g Carbohydrate (trace Fibre, trace Sugar); 3 g Protein; 180 mg Sodium

Some days you just have to give in to your sweet tooth. If it's one of those days, make a sweet cornbread instead: increase sugar to 1/2 cup (125 mL), replace corn kernels with 1 cup (250 mL) fresh or frozen blueberries, and leave out Parmesan, rosemary and black pepper. Bake the same way as this recipe, or in greased muffin tins for a portable snack.

Sweet Potato and Wild Rice Waffles

Makes 16 waffles

These savoury waffles are completely different from the sweet breakfast waffles you're used to. While they don't pair so well with maple syrup or fruit, they make a great healthy snack to eat out of hand, they're delicious with just a little butter as part of breakfast or with soup at lunch, and they're to die for with sour cream and smoked salmon.

3 medium potatoes (about 1 1/2 lb, 680 g), peeled and coarsely grated

1 medium sweet potato (about 1 1/2 lb, 680 g), peeled and coarsely grated

1 Tbsp (15 mL) grape seed oil

6 Tbsp (90 mL) minced shallots

1 1/2 tsp (7 mL) minced garlic

10 eggs

1/2 cup (125 mL) whipping cream (30 percent)

2 cups (500 mL) all-purpose flour

2 Tbsp (30 mL) baking powder

1 Tbsp (15 mL) *each* salt and freshly ground pepper

2 Tbsp (30 mL) chopped chives

6 Tbsp (90 mL) chopped fresh oregano

2 cups (500 mL) cooked wild rice (a little more than 1/2 cup, 125 mL, uncooked)

Bring a large saucepan of water to a boil over medium-high heat. Cook grated potato until tender, about 5 to 6 minutes. Drain. Refresh in ice water. Drain, then squeeze totally dry with paper towel. Repeat with sweet potato, using new water. Set both aside.

Heat oil in a medium sauté pan. Add shallots and garlic. Cook, stirring, until fragrant and softened, about 3 to 5 minutes. Set aside to cool.

In a large bowl, beat eggs with a whisk. Add cream and whisk to combine. In a separate medium bowl, sift together flour and baking powder. Stir in salt, pepper, chives and oregano. Add flour mixture to egg mixture and whisk to combine thoroughly. Add shallot mixture and mix well. Add potatoes, sweet potatoes and wild rice. Mix thoroughly.

Preheat waffle iron and spray with non-stick cooking spray. Ladle the appropriate portion for your model onto waffle iron and spread evenly with a spatula. (For most standard 2-waffle irons, 6 fl oz, 180 mL, is the perfect portion.) Cook 5 to 6 minutes until crisp and golden. Serve immediately.

1 waffle: 210 Calories; 7 g Total Fat (2 g Mono, 1.5 g Poly, 2.5 g Sat); 140 mg Cholesterol; 29 g Carbohydrate (3 g Fibre, 1 g Sugar); 8 g Protein; 140 mg Sodium

Tip

You could easily halve this recipe, but we prefer to make the full batch and freeze extra waffles for homemade toaster waffles. Cook waffles for 4 minutes, until just barely golden brown on the outside. Transfer to a wire rack to cool completely. Wrap tightly in plastic wrap or insert into a resealable freezer bag and freeze for up to 3 months. To reheat, drop frozen waffles into the toaster and toast until puffed, golden and crisp.

Pumpkin Bannock

Makes 2 dozen cakes

Sometimes known as bannock, sometimes as frybread, this simple bread was made in hundreds of variations by early settlers and First Nations people. Originally unleavened, now leavened with baking powder, bannock can be savoury or sweet. Here, we offer a sweet version flavoured with an autumn favourite.

2 cups (500 mL) pumpkin purée (see Tip)

1/2 cup (125 mL) plus 1 Tbsp (15 mL) sugar, *divided*

1/4 tsp (1 mL) vanilla

3 cups (750 mL) all-purpose flour

4 tsp (20 mL) baking powder

1 tsp (5 mL) baking soda

1/4 tsp (1 mL) cinnamon

1/4 tsp (1 mL) nutmeg

1/2 cup (125 mL) water

vegetable oil, for frying

In a medium bowl, mix pumpkin purée with 1/2 cup (125 mL) sugar and vanilla until well combined.

In another medium bowl, sift flour, baking powder, baking soda and spices. Add pumpkin mixture and water and mix until it just comes together to form a soft dough. Cut dough into 4 equal parts. Pinch off small pieces and form into individual cakes about 2 inches (5 cm) across and 1 inch (2.5 cm) thick.

Pour oil into a large, deep sauté pan until 1 inch (2.5 cm) deep. Heat over medium-high. Working in batches, fry cakes until golden brown on one side. Flip and brown the other side. The cakes will puff up as they cook. With a slotted spoon, transfer cakes to paper towels to drain. Sprinkle with remaining sugar.

1 cake: 100 Calories; 2.5 g Total Fat (1.5 g Mono, 0.5 g Poly, 0 g Sat); 0 mg Cholesterol; 18 g Carbohydrate (1 g Fibre, 5 g Sugar); 2 g Protein; 15 mg Sodium

Tip

To make your own pumpkin purée, preheat oven to 350°F (175°C). Cut a slice off the bottom of the pumpkin to make it sit flat, and then cut off the stem end. Using a large knife, cut off all the skin. Cut in half or in quarters. Scrape out the seeds and pulp with a spoon. Place pumpkin pieces in a baking dish and add just enough water to cover the bottom of the pan. Bake until the flesh is tender and pierced easily with a fork, about 45 minutes to 1 hour, or more, depending on the size of the pumpkin. Drain off any remaining liquid and set aside to cool. Purée in a food processor until smooth.

Apple and Cranberry Crostata

Serves 7

This free-form pie offers a casually elegant alternative to traditional apple pie, and makes delicious use of two of our most prolific autumn fruits. You will need a pastry or bench scraper and an 11 inch (28 cm) springform or round fluted tart pan (at least 1 1/4 inches, 3 cm, deep) with removable bottom.

4 or 5 Gala or Fuji apples (about 2 lbs, 900 g)

2 Tbsp (30 mL) lemon juice

3/4 cup (175 mL) plus 3 Tbsp (45 mL) sugar, *divided*

1 Tbsp (15 mL) cinnamon

1/4 tsp (1 mL) ground cloves

1 cup (250 mL) cranberries

2 cups (500 mL) plus 1/4 cup (60 mL) all-purpose flour, *divided*

1 tsp (5 mL) kosher salt

1 cup (250 mL) cold butter, cut into 1/2 inch (12 mm) cubes

6 to 8 Tbsp (90 to 120 mL) ice water

(see next page)

For the filling, peel, quarter and core apples, then cut into 1 inch (2.5 cm) chunks. Combine apples and lemon juice in a large sauté pan. Toss. Add 3/4 cup (175 mL) sugar, cinnamon and cloves. Cook, stirring occasionally, over medium heat until mixture starts to soften, about 30 minutes. Add cranberries and cook until apples and cranberries are soft and apples are starting to caramelize, another 20 to 30 minutes. Remove from heat and cool at room temperature.

Make pastry shell while fruit cooks. In a large bowl, sift together 2 cups (500 mL) flour, kosher salt and 2 Tbsp (30 mL) sugar. Blend in cold butter with your fingertips or a pastry blender until mixture resembles coarse meal with some roughly pea-size butter lumps. Drizzle evenly with 6 Tbsp (90 mL) ice water and gently stir with a fork until incorporated. Squeeze a small handful: if dough doesn't hold together, add more ice water, 1 Tbsp (15 mL) at a time, stirring until just combined.

Turn out dough onto lightly floured surface and divide into 6 portions. With the heel of your hand, smear each portion once or twice in a forward motion to help distribute fat. Gather all the dough together with scraper and press into a ball, then flatten into a disk. Chill dough, wrapped tightly in plastic wrap, until firm, at least 1 hour.

Roll out chilled dough on lightly floured surface with a lightly floured rolling pin into a 14 inch (35.5 cm) round, then fit into springform or tart pan (do not trim).

Put a large baking sheet on centre rack of oven and preheat oven to 375°F (190°C).

For filling, cream together softened butter and sugars in a mixer or large bowl until pale and fluffy. Add eggs one at a time, beating well after each addition, then beat in vanilla. Add 1/4 cup (60 mL) flour and 1/8 tsp (0.5 mL) salt, and mix until just combined.

To assemble, spread brown sugar mixture evenly over pastry. Scatter cooked fruit with juices over filling. Fold edge of pastry over filling to partially cover (centre won't be covered). Pleat dough as necessary. Brush folded pastry edge lightly with egg and sprinkle with sugar.

Bake on preheated baking sheet until filling is puffed and set and pastry is golden brown, 50 to 60 minutes. Cool, about 1 1/2 hours. Remove side of springform or tart pan and slide crostata onto plate to serve. Serve warm, with ice cream if you like.

1 serving: 550 Calories; 30 g Total Fat (8 g Mono, 1.5 g Poly, 18 g Sat); 135 mg Cholesterol; 69 g Carbohydrate (4 g Fibre, 43 g Sugar); 5 g Protein; 470 mg Sodium

1/2 cup (125 mL) butter, softened

1/2 cup (125 mL) packed light brown sugar

1/2 cup (125 mL) icing sugar

2 large eggs

1 tsp (5 mL) vanilla

1/8 tsp (0.5 mL) salt

1 large egg, lightly beaten

Applesauce Loaf

Serves 7

People have been eating apples since the Iron Age, and in Canada, we've been growing them since the arrival of the first European settlers in the 1600s. They dried apples for year-round use in pies, puddings and other desserts. Canning applesauce was another way to preserve the harvest to use throughout the year. Here, Cinnamon-Calvados Applesauce is baked into a succulent, moist loaf, accented with dried blueberries. You could change it up by substituting plain applesauce other dried fruits such as apricot (chopped), cranberries, currants or raisins.

1/2 cup (125 mL) butter, softened

1 cup (250 mL) sugar

1 egg

1 1/2 cups (375 mL) all-purpose flour

1 1/2 tsp (7 mL) baking soda

1 tsp (5 mL) cinnamon

3/4 tsp (4 mL) nutmeg

1/2 tsp (2 mL) ground cloves

1/2 tsp (2 mL) salt

1 1/4 cups (300 mL) Cinnamon-Calvados Applesauce

1/2 cup (125 mL) dried blueberries

icing sugar, if desired

Preheat oven to 350°F (175°C). In a mixer or medium bowl, cream butter and sugar until light. Beat in egg.

In a separate medium bowl, sift together flour, baking soda, cinnamon, nutmeg, cloves and salt. Add in 3 batches to butter mixture, mixing well after each addition. Add applesauce and mix thoroughly. Stir in dried blueberries. Pour into a greased and floured 8 1/2 x 4 1/2 inch (21 x 11 cm) loaf pan. Bake 1 hour. Cool in pan 10 minutes. Remove from pan and cool on wire rack. Sprinkle with icing sugar if desired. Keep tightly wrapped at room temperature for up to 3 days.

1 slice: 430 Calories; 15 g Total Fat (1.5 g Mono, 0.5 g Poly, 9 g Sat); 65 mg Cholesterol; 74 g Carbohydrate (3 g Fibre, 51 g Sugar); 3 g Protein; 550 mg Sodium

Cinnamon-Calvados Applesauce

Makes 1 1/4 cups (300 mL)

Cut apples into 1 inch (2.5 cm) pieces. Combine apples, water, sugar, zest and cinnamon in medium saucepan. Bring to a boil, then cover and reduce heat to medium. Cook, stirring occasionally, until apples are tender, about 15 minutes. Remove lid. Continue cooking, stirring occasionally, until most of the liquid has evaporated. Stir in Calvados. Cook 1 minute more. Remove from heat. Stir in lemon juice. Mash with a potato masher or fork for a chunky applesauce, or purée in a food processor for a smoother sauce. Cool, uncovered, at room temperature. Keep covered and refrigerated for up to 3 days.

1/4 cup (60 mL): 120 Calories; 0 g Total Fat (0 g Mono, 0 g Poly, 0 g Sat); 0 mg Cholesterol; 27 g Carbohydrate (2 g Fibre, 24 g Sugar); 0 g Protein; 5 mg Sodium

1 lb (454 g) apples (try Gala, Fuji and Golden Delicious), peeled and cored

1/2 cup (125 mL) water

1/3 cup (90 mL) golden brown sugar

1/2 tsp (2 mL) finely grated lemon zest

pinch of cinnamon

2 Tbsp (30 mL) Calvados

2 1/2 tsp (12 mL) lemon juice

Quince and Apple Strudel

Serves 9

Apples and quince are cousins and have often been interchangeable in folklore. Both were said to be ritual wedding items in ancient Greece, and some historians believe the apple of knowledge in the garden of Eden was actually a quince. Quince were brought to North America at the same time as apples, but apples soon eclipsed them in popularity because of the apple's smoother, more appealing exterior, and the fact that they could be eaten out of hand, while quince must be cooked before eating. The two cousins are happily reunited in this strudel.

2 Fuji or Gala apples

2 quince

1/4 cup (60 mL) plus 2 Tbsp (30 mL) sugar, *divided*

2 Tbsp (30 mL) fresh lemon juice

2 Tbsp (30 mL) minced ginger root

2 x 3 inch (7.5 cm) cinnamon sticks

4 whole cloves

3/4 cup (175 mL) toasted almonds

20 gingersnap cookies

10 sheets phyllo pastry

1 cup (250 mL) butter, melted

Preheat oven to 375°F (190°C). Peel, core and quarter apples and quince. Cut each quarter into 2 or 3 slices, no more than 1/2 inch (12 mm) thick. In a large bowl, toss apples and quince with 1/4 cup (60 mL) sugar, lemon juice, ginger, cinnamon sticks and cloves. Spread out in a single layer in a greased shallow baking dish. Roast, stirring occasionally, until fruit is soft and caramelized, about 1 to 1 1/4 hours. Remove from oven. Discard cinnamon sticks and cloves. Cool in pan on wire rack until room temperature, about 45 minutes.

Finely grind almonds, gingersnaps and 2 Tbsp (30 mL) sugar in food processor. Transfer to a small bowl.

Butter baking sheet. Place a clean kitchen towel on a work surface. Place 1 phyllo sheet on towel. Keep remaining phyllo sheets covered with plastic wrap and a damp kitchen towel while you work. Brush phyllo sheet with butter. Top with a second phyllo sheet. Brush with butter. Sprinkle with 3 Tbsp (45 mL) of almond mixture. Continue layering phyllo sheets, brushing each with butter and sprinkling with almond mixture. Top with final phyllo sheet and brush with butter.

Beginning 2 inches (5 cm) in from one long side and
2 1/2 inches (6.4 cm) in from one short side, spoon fruit
filling in a 3 inch (7.5 cm) wide by 12 inch (30 cm) long log
parallel to one long side. Fold short sides over filling.
Brush folded edges with butter. Using the towel, start at
one long side to roll up strudel, enclosing filling. With a
large spatula, transfer to prepared baking sheet. Brush
with butter. (The strudel can be made up to this point
4 hours ahead. Cover with plastic wrap and chill until
ready to bake.)

Preheat oven to 375°F (190°C). Set baking sheet with strudel
on top of a second baking sheet. Bake strudel until golden
brown, about 45 minutes. Let stand at least 15 minutes and
up to 4 hours before serving. To serve, slice crosswise into
1 inch (2.5 cm) thick slices.

*1 serving: 450 Calories; 27 g Total Fat (9 g Mono, 2 g Poly,
14 g Sat); 55 mg Cholesterol; 43 g Carbohydrate (4 g Fibre,
18 g Sugar); 6 g Protein; 400 mg Sodium*

Gingerbread Waffles

Makes 8 waffles

Can you think of a better way to spend an autumn Sunday morning than lingering over a homemade brunch before heading outside to enjoy the fresh air? These gingerbread waffles are a wonderful seasonal twist on the classic. But they're not just for breakfast—they're delicious with vanilla ice cream for dessert, too.

3 cups (750 mL) all-purpose flour

1 cup (250 mL) packed dark brown sugar

1 Tbsp (15 mL) baking powder

1 1/2 tsp (7 mL) baking soda

1 tsp (5 mL) salt

2 tsp (10 mL) cinnamon

2 tsp (10 mL) ground ginger

1/2 tsp (2 mL) ground nutmeg

1/4 tsp (1 mL) ground cloves

1/4 cup (60 mL) molasses (not blackstrap)

3/4 cup (175 mL) water

4 large eggs

1/2 cup (125 mL) butter, melted and cooled

1/4 cup (60 mL) fresh lemon or lime juice

Preheat waffle iron and spray with non-stick cooking spray. In a large bowl, whisk together flour, brown sugar, baking powder, baking soda, salt and spices. In a second large bowl, whisk together molasses, water, eggs, butter and lemon juice. Add flour mixture and whisk until just combined. Let stand 15 minutes (batter will thicken). Add a little water to thin to proper consistency, keeping it a little on the thick side.

Ladle about 1/2 cup (125 mL) batter into waffle iron and spread gently with a spatula. Cook until crisp, about 4 minutes.

1 waffle: 450 Calories; 15 g Total Fat (4 g Mono, 1 g Poly, 8 g Sat); 135 mg Cholesterol; 72 g Carbohydrate (2 g Fibre, 34 g Sugar); 8 g Protein; 490 mg Sodium

Tip

This batter is thinner than the batter in the Sweet Potato
and Wild Rice Waffles (p. 132) and will rise more in a
standard waffle iron, so less of it is required.

Gingerbread Bread Puddings

Serves 8

The smell of gingerbread wafting through the house is a celebration of autumn, hinting at all the culinary delights of the season. With this recipe, you'll get to enjoy the delicious aromas twice over—when you bake the cake, and again when you bake the puddings. The cake is delicious in its original form, too: try it with some stewed fruit or a little ice cream (or both) on the side. You will need a springform pan for the Gingerbread Cake.

1 cup (250 mL) dark molasses

1 tsp (5 mL) baking soda

1 1/2 cups (375 mL) boiling water

1/2 cup (125 mL) butter

1 1/4 cups (310 mL) packed brown sugar

7 eggs, *divided*

3 cups (750 mL) all-purpose flour

1 Tbsp (15 mL) baking powder

5 tsp (25 mL) ground ginger

1 1/4 tsp (6 mL) cinnamon

1/8 tsp (0.5 mL) ground cloves

1/2 tsp (2 mL) plus 1/8 tsp (0.5 mL) salt

(see next page)

For the cake, preheat oven to 300°F (150°C). In large bowl, combine molasses and baking soda with water. Stir until well combined. Cool to room temperature.

In a mixer or large bowl, cream butter and brown sugar until light and fluffy. Add 1 egg and mix until incorporated.

In a second large bowl, sift together flour, baking powder, 4 tsp (20 mL) ginger, cinnamon, cloves and 1/2 tsp (2 mL) salt. Beginning and ending with dry ingredients, add dry ingredients and molasses mixture to batter, in several batches. Transfer batter to greased 10 inch (25 cm) springform pan. Bake until a toothpick inserted into centre comes out clean, about 35 to 45 minutes. Cool in pan on a wire rack. Once cooled completely, remove from pan. Cut in half. Wrap one half tightly in plastic wrap and reserve for another use. Set second half aside, uncovered, at room temperature overnight.

Cut gingerbread cake into 1/2 inch (12 mm) cubes. Spread out on 2 baking sheets and let sit, uncovered, at room temperature for at least 2 or 3 hours.

For pudding, preheat oven to 325°F (160°C). In a large saucepan combine milk and ginger root. Bring to a boil over medium-high heat. Reduce heat to medium. Simmer, uncovered, 10 minutes.

In a large bowl, beat together eggs and sugar. Whisk in vanilla, 1 tsp (5 mL) ground ginger and 1/8 tsp (0.5 mL) salt until well combined. Gradually whisk in hot milk. Strain into a clean, large bowl.

Loosely pack cake cubes into eight 1 cup (250 mL) ramekins (cake cubes can come past the top). Pour custard over top. Let stand 15 minutes. Arrange ramekins in a shallow roasting pan. Pour enough boiling water into roasting pan to reach halfway up sides of ramekins. Bake until set, until a knife inserted in centre comes out clean, about 1 hour.

1 serving: 480 Calories; 11 g Total Fat (3 g Mono, 1 g Poly, 6 g Sat); 190 mg Cholesterol; 83 g Carbohydrate (trace Fibre, 61 g Sugar); 13 Protein; 460 mg Sodium

4 cups (1 L) milk

1 x 2 inch (5 cm) piece of ginger root, peeled and minced

1 cup (250 mL) sugar

2 tsp (10 mL) vanilla

1 tsp (5 mL) ground ginger

pinch of salt

Hazelnut Crème Brûlée

Serves 6

Would crème brûlée by any other name taste as sweet? It probably would, but "burnt cream" is certainly a much less appealing moniker. Several countries claim it as their own, but credit goes to the French for popularizing it. You'll see endless variations of this dish on restaurant dessert menus, but you may be surprised to discover how easy it is to make at home. A kitchen blowtorch is a handy piece of equipment to have for this recipe (see Tip).

6 large egg yolks

1/4 cup (60 mL) plus 3 Tbsp (45 mL) sugar, *divided*

2 1/4 cups (550 mL) whipping cream (30 percent)

2 Tbsp (30 mL) Frangelico

2 tsp (10 mL) vanilla extract

berry sugar for sprinkling

Preheat oven to 325°F (160°C). Whisk egg yolks and sugar in medium bowl until thick and pale yellow, about 2 minutes. Bring cream to a simmer in a small saucepan. Gradually whisk hot cream into yolk mixture. Whisk in Frangelico and vanilla; divide custard among six 3/4 cup (175 mL) custard cups. Arrange cups in 13 x 9 x 2 inch (33 x 23 x 5 cm) metal pan. Pour enough hot water into pan to come halfway up sides of cups. Bake custards until barely set in centre, about 25 minutes. Remove cups from water and refrigerate, uncovered, until cold, at least 3 hours. The custards can be made a day ahead up to this point.

Sprinkle berry sugar in an even layer over surface of each custard. Use your blowtorch to melt and caramelize the sugar until it turns golden brown and starts to bubble. Serve within 2 to 3 hours.

1 serving: 420 Calories; 33 g Total Fat (10 g Mono, 1.5 g Poly, 20 g Sat); 315 mg Cholesterol; 26 g Carbohydrate (0 g Fibre, 23 g Sugar); 5 g Protein; 40 mg Sodium

Tip

If you don't have a blowtorch, melt 3/4 cup (175 mL) sugar in a small saucepan over medium-high heat. Use a clean pastry brush dipped in water to dissolve any crystals that stick to the sides of the pan. Once all the sugar melts, do not stir. Heat until the syrup caramelizes and turns light golden brown. Remove from heat and carefully pour a layer of syrup over each custard cup.

Cranberry Tartlets

Serves 8

Cranberries are often relegated to a supporting role as a tart side dish spread onto the main feature. Nestled in a sweet, creamy Mascarpone filling, these autumn jewels shine in the dessert course.

1 tsp (5 mL) gelatin

1/2 cup (125 mL) cranberry juice, *divided*

1 x 12 oz (340 g) bag cranberries

3/4 cup (175 mL) sugar

3 tsp (30 mL) lemon juice, *divided*

1 tsp (5 mL) finely grated lemon zest

1 tsp (5 mL) grated ginger root

1/8 tsp (0.5 mL) salt

1 cup (250 mL) all-purpose flour

1 cup (250 mL) icing sugar, *divided*

1/2 tsp (2 mL) plus 1/8 tsp (0.5 mL) salt

1/2 cup (125 mL) cold butter, cut into 1/2 inch (12 mm) cubes

1 large egg yolk

2 Tbsp (30 mL) ice water

(see next page)

For the topping, in a small bowl, soften gelatin in 1/4 cup (60 mL) cranberry juice. Let stand 15 minutes.

In a medium saucepan, combine remaining 1/4 cup (60 mL) cranberry juice, cranberries, sugar, 2 tsp (10 mL) lemon juice and zest, ginger and salt. Bring to a boil, stirring until sugar has dissolved. Reduce heat to medium. Simmer until cranberries are tender, about 5 minutes. Strain juice into a medium bowl. Set cranberries aside. Add gelatin mixture to hot juice. Stir until gelatin has dissolved. Add cranberries to juice. Stir to combine. Chill until cold and slightly thickened, at least 8 hours or overnight. (The topping can be made up to 2 days ahead and kept, covered, in the refrigerator.)

For the tart shells, combine flour, 1/2 cup (125 mL) icing sugar and 1/2 tsp (2 mL) salt in a food processor. Pulse together. Add butter. Pulse until mixture resembles coarse meal. In a small bowl, combine egg yolk, water and 1 tsp (5 mL) lemon juice. Add to processor. Pulse until pea-size lumps form and dough holds together when squeezed.

Lightly flour your hands. Press 1/4 cup (60 mL) dough into each round tartlet pan. Prick bottoms with a fork. Chill until firm, about 20 minutes.

Preheat oven to 325°F (160°C). Put shells on a baking sheet. Bake in lower third of oven until golden, about 20 to 25 minutes. Transfer to a wire rack to cool. When just cool enough to handle, loosen edges carefully with a knife and remove shells from pans. (Tart shells can be made up to 2 days ahead and stored in an airtight container at room temperature.)

For the filling, combine Mascarpone cheese, 1/2 cup (125 mL) icing sugar, whipping cream and vanilla in a mixer or large bowl. Beat until well combined and just thick enough to spread. Do not overbeat. (Filling can be made up to a day ahead.)

To assemble, spread filling in cooled crusts. Spoon cranberry mixture evenly over filling. Serve cold.

1 tartlet: *460 Calories; 27 g Total Fat (4.5 g Mono, 0.5 g Poly, 18 g Sat); 110 mg Cholesterol; 50 g Carbohydrate (2 g Fibre, 35 g Sugar); 4 g Protein; 280 mg Sodium*

8 oz (225 g) Mascarpone cheese

1/2 cup (125 mL) chilled whipping cream (30 percent)

1 tsp (5 mL) vanilla

Gingered Pear Tarte Tatin

Serves 8

According to culinary legend, tarte tatin was invented by happy accident when Stephanie Tatin dropped her apple tart onto the floor on the way to the oven. In an effort to rescue it, she put the apples back into the pan and laid the pastry overtop, then turned it upside down to serve it. Our recipe replaces apples with pears, but keeps the elegant presentation of the original.

1/2 cup (125 mL) butter

1 thumb-size knob of ginger, peeled and finely grated

3/4 cup (75 mL) sugar

1/8 tsp (0.5 mL) salt

1 tsp (5 mL) vanilla

6 to 8 firm pears, halved and cored (not peeled), reserved in acidulated water (see p. 39)

pastry for a single crust pie, chilled (see Great Pie Crust, opposite)

Melt butter in 10 inch (25 cm) ovenproof sauté pan over medium-low heat. Add ginger and cook until fragrant, about 1 minute, stirring often. Add sugar, salt and vanilla. Stir gently until sugar has melted. Cook, without stirring, until it turns a rich caramel colour. Remove from heat.

Starting at outer edge of pan, lay pear halves, cut side up, to form concentric circles, packing as close together as possible. Return pan to stove over medium heat, and cook until pears begin to release their juices, 3 to 5 minutes. Increase heat to medium-high and cook until pears are just tender and caramelized on bottom edge, 10 to 15 minutes, then flip each pear half and cook other side until caramelized. Remove from heat and let cool in pan to room temperature. If there's more than 1/2 inch (12 mm) of liquid in pan, carefully pour off and reserve the excess.

Preheat oven to 375°F (190°C). Roll out pie dough into an 11 inch (28 cm) round. Drape dough over pears tucking edge under to make a rim. Place pan on a baking sheet and bake until crust is crisp and golden brown, about 25 minutes.

Let cool 15 minutes. Carefully pour off and reserve pan juices with the juices reserved earlier, if any. If reserved juices are thin, simmer over medium-low heat until thick enough to coat the back of a spoon.

Invert a plate over tarte and flip over, then lift off pan. Serve warm or at room temperature with vanilla ice cream; drizzle caramelized juices overtop. Leftovers won't keep more than a day or so and shouldn't be refrigerated.

1 serving: 510 Calories; 29 g Total Fat (8 g Mono, 1 g Poly,1 g Sat); 18 mg Cholesterol; 63 g Carbohydrate (6 g Fibre, 37 g Sugar); 3 g Protein; 380 mg Sodium

Great Pie Crust

Makes 1 double-crusted pie

Mix flour, salt and sugar in a bowl. Using your cheese grater, grate frozen butter into flour mixture. Toss lightly to distribute butter, and add lemon juice and just enough water for dough to come together. Divide in half, wrap each piece in plastic wrap and flatten into a disc. Chill for at least 30 minutes before using.

Per 1/16: 180 Calories; 12 g Total Fat (3 g Mono, 0.5 g Poly, 7 g Sat); 30 mg Cholesterol; 16 g Carbohydrate (trace Fibre, trace Sugar); 2 g Protein; 220 mg Sodium

2 1/2 cups (625 mL) all-purpose flour

1 tsp (5mL) sea salt

1 Tbsp (15 mL) sugar

1 cup (250 mL) unsalted butter, frozen

1 Tbsp (15 mL) lemon juice

about 1/3 cup (75 mL) ice water

Pumpkin Mousse

Serves 7

If you love pumpkin pie, wait until you try this mousse. Rich with pumpkin and spice flavours, yet light and airy at the same time, this mousse offers an elegant, melt-in-your-mouth twist on a seasonal classic.

1 tsp (5 mL) gelatin

2 Tbsp (30 mL) cold water

4 egg yolks

1 cup (250 mL) sugar

2 Tbsp (30 mL) cold water

2 cups (500 mL) pumpkin purée (see p. 135)

2 Tbsp (30 mL) brandy or Calvados

1 tsp (5 mL) cinnamon

1/2 tsp (2 mL) ginger

1/4 tsp (1 mL) cloves

1 3/4 cups (425 mL) whipping cream (30 percent)

1 Tbsp (15 mL) vanilla

In a small bowl soften gelatin in first amount of cold water.

In a medium metal bowl over a pot of simmering water, combine egg yolks, sugar and second amount of cold water. Whisk constantly until it doubles in volume and holds a ribbon when whisk is lifted, about 5 minutes. Remove from heat and stir in gelatin.

Transfer to a mixer fitted with a whisk attachment and beat until cooled, another 5 minutes. Fold in pumpkin, brandy and spices and chill until cool but not set, about 30 minutes.

While base is chilling, whip cream to soft peaks and add vanilla. Fold into mousse in 2 batches. Transfer to a serving dishes and chill until ready to serve.

1 serving: 350 Calories; 22 g Total Fat (7 g Mono, 1 g Poly, 13 g Sat); 190 mg Cholesterol; 36 g Carbohydrate (3 g Fibre, 31 g Sugar); 4 g Protein; 30 mg Sodium

Maple Walnut Shortbread

Makes 8 wedges

Scottish folklore says that the traditional round shortbread cut into wedges was baked in the darker months to represent the sun's rays. Here in Canada, our winters rival those of Scotland, so it's no wonder that every family of Scottish heritage in Canada has its own recipe for shortbread. We don't want to compete with Grandma, but ours adds a Canadian twist with the addition of maple syrup.

1/2 cup (125 mL) cold, unsalted butter, cut into 1/2 inch (12 mm) cubes

3 Tbsp (45 mL) packed dark brown sugar

2 Tbsp (30 mL) maple syrup

3 Tbsp (45 mL) sugar, *divided*

1 tsp (5 mL) vanilla

3/4 cup (175 mL) plus 2 Tbsp (30 mL) all-purpose flour

2 Tbsp (30 mL) cornstarch

1/4 tsp (1 mL) salt

1/4 cup (60 mL) coarsely chopped toasted walnuts

Preheat oven to 350°F (190°C). Put a 9 inch (23 cm) tart pan with a removable bottom in freezer to chill.

Cream butter, brown sugar, maple syrup, 1 Tbsp (15 mL) sugar and vanilla in mixer or medium bowl and mix just until smooth, about 30 seconds. Sift flour, cornstarch and salt in small bowl. Stir in walnuts. Add dry ingredients to butter mixture and mix just until clumps form.

Press evenly into chilled pan, then sprinkle evenly with 2 Tbsp (30 mL) sugar. Prick all over with a fork and freeze for 5 minutes.

Bake in middle rack of oven until edges are golden, 25 to 30 minutes. Cool in pan on rack for 5 minutes and, while still warm, cut into 8 wedges. Cool completely before removing from pan. Keep in an airtight container at room temperature for up to 5 days.

1 wedge: 230 Calories; 14 g Total Fat (3.5 g Mono, 2 g Poly, 8 g Sat); 30 mg Cholesterol; 25 g Carbohydrate (trace Fibre, 12 g Sugar); 2 g Protein; 160 mg Sodium

Shortbread is so familiar to most of us that we don't stop to think about its name. But why "shortbread"? "Short" because the high fat content of the dough hinders gluten development, producing a "short" dough that when baked has a crumbly texture (pie pastry is also a short dough). The "bread" part is less clear, but according to folklore, early Scottish bakers wanted to avoid having shortbread classified as a biscuit because biscuits were subject to government taxes.

Hazelnut Biscotti

Makes 3 dozen biscotti

Biscotti literally means "twice baked." This hard, dry cookie is not meant to be eaten out of hand—it's made for dipping in cappuccino (or just plain coffee), tea, hot chocolate or even wine. Biscotti were originally almond-flavoured, but the possibilities for variation are endless. Ours packs the punch of whole hazelnuts.

2 1/2 cups (625 mL) all-purpose flour

1 Tbsp (15 mL) baking powder

1/2 tsp (2 mL) salt

1/4 tsp (1 mL) cinnamon

1/4 tsp (1 mL) ground cloves

1/4 tsp (1 mL) nutmeg

1/2 cup (125 mL) unsalted butter, at room temperature

1 cup (250 mL) sugar

2 tsp (10 mL) vanilla extract

3 large eggs

1 cup (250 mL) hazelnuts, toasted and husked

2 oz (57 g) semi-sweet baking chocolate

Preheat oven to 350°F (175°C). Spray large baking sheet with non-stick cooking spray.

Mix flour, baking powder, salt and spices in a medium bowl and set aside. Cream butter and sugar in a mixer or large bowl until fluffy. Add vanilla extract and mix well. Add eggs one at a time, mixing just until incorporated after each addition. Add flour mixture. Mix until just combined. Add hazelnuts and mix just until evenly distributed throughout the dough.

Turn dough out onto floured work surface. Divide in half. Roll each half into a 9 inch (23 cm) long, 2 inch (5 cm) wide log. Space logs 3 inches (7.5 cm) apart on prepared baking sheet. Flatten each to a 12 inch (30 cm) long, 2 1/2 inch (6.4 cm) wide log. Bake until light golden and firm to touch, about 25 minutes. Cool on baking sheet 5 minutes. Reduce oven temperature to 325°F (160°C).

With a metal spatula, transfer logs to a work surface. Use a serrated knife to cut logs diagonally into 3/4 inch (2 cm) wide slices. Place slices, cut side down, on a large ungreased baking sheet. Bake 15 minutes. Turn biscotti over; bake until light golden and firm, about 15 minutes longer. Transfer biscotti to racks to cool.

Coarsely chop chocolate. Transfer to a small non-metal bowl. Melt in microwave at medium power, checking and stirring after 1 minute increments. Transfer to a parchment paper piping bag. Cut a small hole in tip. Set rack of cookies on baking sheet. Drizzle chocolate back and forth over biscotti. Cool. Store for up to 3 days in an airtight container at room temperature.

1 biscotti: 110 Calories; 6 g Total Fat (2.5 g Mono, 0 g Poly, 2 g Sat); 25 mg Cholesterol; 14 g Carbohydrate (trace Fibre, 7 g Sugar); 2 g Protein; 80 mg Sodium

Cranberry Breeze Punch

Serves 20

Light and refreshing rather than sugary-sweet, this bubbly punch is sure to be a crowd pleaser. The Amaretto adds warmth to the drink but can be left out for a non-alcoholic version. The hot mulled cider is the ideal wrap-up to a chilly afternoon spent raking leaves or bringing in the last of the harvest. The mulling spices will warm you all the way to the tips of your toes.

3 Tbsp (45 mL) sugar

1 cup (250 mL) fresh grapefruit juice

8 cups (2 L) cranberry juice cocktail, chilled

8 cups (2 L) ginger ale, chilled

4 cups (1 L) club soda, chilled

1 cup (250 mL) Amaretto

1 tray ice cubes

frozen cranberries for garnish

In a small bowl, stir sugar into grapefruit juice until completely dissolved. Combine cranberry juice, ginger ale, club soda, Amaretto and grapefruit juice mixture in a punch bowl. Add ice and frozen cranberries, and serve.

1 serving: 150 Calories; 0 g Total Fat (0 g Mono, 0 g Poly, 0 g Sat); 0 mg Cholesterol; 35 g Carbohydrate (0 g Fibre, 35 g Sugar); 0 g Protein; 10 mg Sodium

Mulled Cranberry Apple Cider

Serves 8

Heat a large saucepan over medium-high. Add cinnamon sticks, peppercorns and cloves to dry pan. Cook, tossing occasionally, until fragrant, 1 or 2 minutes. Add apple cider and cranberry juice. Increase heat to high and bring to a boil. Stir in brown sugar to dissolve. Reduce heat to medium-low. Once cider has come down to a simmer, add zest. Simmer, partially covered, for about 30 minutes. Remove from heat. Pour through a fine-mesh sieve into a serving vessel of your choice.

1 serving: *120 Calories; 0 g Total Fat (0 g Mono, 0 g Poly, 0 g Sat); 0 mg Cholesterol; 24 g Carbohydrate (0 g Fibre, 23 g Sugar); 0 g Protein; 15 mg Sodium*

2 x 3 inch (7.5 cm) cinnamon sticks

30 whole black peppercorns

6 whole cloves

6 cups (1.5 L) unfiltered apple cider

2 cups (500 mL) unsweetened cranberry juice

1/4 cup (60 mL) packed brown sugar

finely grated zest of 2 lemons or 1 orange

INDEX